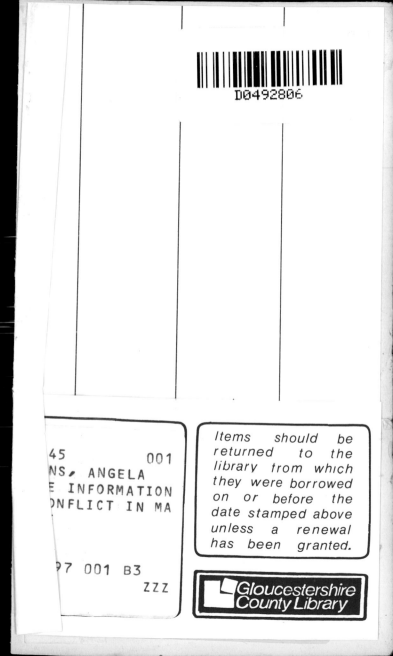

inside information
on conflict in marriage

Angela Willans B.A.
Foreword by J. H. Wallis

The Dickens Press

Published by	The Dickens Press Ltd. 161 Queen Victoria Street, London EC4
Consultant editor	E. Maxwell-Arnot
Designers	Colin Banks and John Miles
Printed by	C. Nicholls & Company Ltd. The Philips Park Press, Manchester

Foreword

Some years ago the Marriage Guidance Council carried out a detailed research into the multitude of problems brought to its counsellors. More than 25,000 cases were recorded and analysed. This project endorsed the experience of journalists that there is almost no limit to the variety of personal problems on which anyone may some day need help, or at least another point of view.

Today, no one is surprised that marriage brings problems. We no longer believe in the myth of perpetual harmony. How can any man and woman (however loving and wise) share their daily lives, their likes and dislikes, their wants and needs, their aims and ideals, their pay-packets without some misunderstandings or argument? Even if that *were* possible, most of us would find such a partnership boring. Marriage is enriched by differences, not by sameness. It is an extraordinary adventure to share life with one of those strange creatures, the other sex. It is sometimes exasperating, sometimes entrancing and always worthwhile.

Twenty years of marriage counselling have taught me one fundamental lesson: that there is no universal formula or recipe to suit everyone. We are all of us incompatible, in the sense of being made differently. Marriage is therefore more a voyage of discovery (and self-discovery) than a primrose path or bed of roses. There are surprises round every corner, provided we are alive to them. Problems are challenges. What matters is not so much how they arise but how we deal with them. Sometimes our resources are taxed, with a vengeance. Minor bothers can grow into major difficulties if we do not come to terms with them.

In this warm, clear and friendly book, Angela Willans looks at a representative assortment of marriage problems that may come the way of anyone. They can lead to a deeper and richer mutual understanding. Or they can fester and become major troubles. What makes the difference?

One decisive factor is surely to be able to see another point of view than one's own – or even to realise that there is one. It is not a matter of who is right but of finding a compromise or perhaps an acceptance of a difference. But that is not always easy. How can it be achieved?

I believe there are two ways. The first is through personal discussion with someone trained in the painstaking and difficult art of counselling. The other is through self-help.

It is in this second way that Mrs Willans's book can be so

helpful. It will help anyone wanting to make the most of marriage, through widening their understanding of its complications and offering fresh ideas. The author's long experience of other people's worries and problems has given her a wide sympathy and practical approach to what can be done or could be done.

Every week several thousand men and women write to advice columns of the popular and successful women's magazines. Only a tiny fraction of these letters can be printed. They contain every sort of problem that can puzzle or perplex us in our closest relationships. And many of the writers could never bring themselves to discuss their difficulties face to face with a counsellor.

In these pages that follow, the reader will not find magic or infallible cures for disharmony, because there are none. Instead, there are practical suggestions that have proved helpful to very many troubled people. New ideas are put forward with sympathy and sense, for the reader to adopt if he (or she) wishes. Where problems are likely to need specialised help or guidance, this is explained. No one can read these pages without feeling encouraged by the intelligent freshness with which familiar situations are considered.

J. H. Wallis

Contents

Introduction

What makes a marriage happy or unhappy? Why do some succeed and others fail? Why are some marriages plagued with problems and others have none (or, at least, none the partners can't cope with).

What, in short, *goes on* in a marriage?

All these questions have been asked, written about and studied more over the past ten years or so than any other questions about the human condition. And, through their work in helping married couples in difficulties, doctors, social workers, psychiatrists and counsellors have been able to see more clearly what actually does go on between men and women attempting to live happily together and bring up their families in harmony.

So have they found the answers?

They have found millions of answers – as many answers, in fact, as there are married couples. For the most important point which emerged, put simply, is this – that the causes of difficulties and their solutions have very, very little to do with *facts* about a marriage, like the husband's income, or housing problems or the stresses and strains of everyday life.

Instead, they found that it is the *feelings* and hopes and fears of the two people in the marriage which make it succeed or fail. Happy people make happy marriages, no matter what events batter at them from outside.

And unhappy people, at war with themselves, bring this battle into marriage and continue it, no matter how favourable their circumstances.

There are not, in fact, any 'marriage problems'. It's the people in the marriage who have problems. The problems come, not from the fact of being married but from the internal struggles of the individual partners to love and be loved, overcome old fears and disappointments, and fulfil their personal dreams.

This, of course, makes every marriage different from any other marriage. It differs because it consists of two unique individuals relating to each other. So we can't really talk about 'marriage problems' just like that. There are *your* marriage problems, and his and hers, and mine. They need *your* answers to solve them and no one else's will quite do.

So, instead of looking to rules and books of instruction or dos and donts about marriage we need to turn inwards and look inside at the relationship, at the inner feelings which are the source of the trouble.

This has been perfectly put as the need of husband and wife 'to listen to their own natures, so that they can understand within themselves what is happening'.

Why then offer you a book of answers to marriage problems?

Well, of course, people can be helped to 'listen to their own natures'. This is precisely what marriage counsellors and other helpers do, if they are good at their jobs. And it is what I have tried to do in this book.

That's why you'll find a reluctance to say 'do this' or 'do that', although sometimes I have said these things. Instead you'll find more appeals to 'ask yourself so-and-so' or to 'find out what you/he/she feels about this.'

I would have liked to ask a lot of questions. But a questionnaire wouldn't have helped much. You must put your own questions in: 'Am I like that?'; 'Is this what's happening with us?'; 'Could this be the reason for our trouble?' and so on.

You mustn't take any answers or advice without turning them over, which means a lot of self-questioning, until you feel in your very bones that it fits you. Listen, or read, try it for size, talk about it with your husband or wife and then, if it fits, use it.

I know that you won't like some of the answers because they stir up feelings and assumptions that you don't particularly want to examine too closely. Others may annoy you a little because they help you to look at another point of view, perhaps when you are feeling hurt or angry and need to feel that your point of view is the only one there is.

Well, that's natural. There *is* a lot of discomfort in trying to put a problem right and getting to the reasons for it and I certainly never underestimate the courage of anyone who knows there is something wrong and is determined to put it right.

It's so much easier, very often, to just blame the other person and jog on with the feeling that you 'picked a loser' and there's nothing you can do about it.

There are a lot of marriages like that, but I hope this book will help you to make sure that yours isn't one of them.

You will find the book divided into Parts, each of which has a short introduction explaining what the Part is about.

But it is not very easy to separate feelings into pigeon-holes, as you can with facts and figures. So you will probably find that your problem may be dealt with under more than one heading. Where different Points cut across each other in this way, I have given cross-references in the text to other relevant Points by their numbers.

I have made references throughout the book to further reading and to agencies and people who help couples with their problems. You will find these, together with other suggestions for reading or help, collected together in Appendix A – *Helping Agencies*, and Appendix B – *Further Reading*, at the back of the book.

You can probably best locate your particular problem by referring to the list of Points at the front of the book, but the index is a further guide.

A last word. I haven't set out to give cosy reassurances because I've found that this isn't any help at all in the long run. And I can't pretend that every problem in life or in marriage *has* an answer.

But I hope this book encourages you to help yourself, to know yourself and your partner as well as you can, to see what could be done about any problem that's worrying you – and to take action.

part i
The Personal Relationship

Marriage, of course, *is* a personal relationship. It is other things too, like a legal contract, and a social unit and the basis of family life. But, as I hope you gathered from the introduction, most people who have had anything to do with marriages in trouble have discovered that to find the answers to any problems in marriage you have to go back to the two people in the marriage and the way they feel about each other and what 'goes on' between them.

So this Part is about the problems of getting along with your life-partner and how you might see more clearly what each of you is needing from the other – and provide it.

1 The dreams of married bliss . . .

One of the most useful things to do when you get the feeling that, as a relationship with someone, your marriage is dissatisfying, empty, uncomfortable or downright painful is to sit down and ask yourself honestly: 'But what, in fact, did I expect from it?'

I'm not implying by this that there is any future in expecting marriage to be a soul-destroying trap. That would be one sure way of turning it into such a trap. But it can be very useful to get quite clear in our minds whether or not we had some unrealistic expectations of marriage which simply could not stand up to reality and which might account for the letdown feeling.

There's no doubt, you see, that most of us, especially women, are conditioned by fiction, advertising and tradition to believe that marriage in itself is the fulfilment of all our dreams and longings.

As adolescents we have visions of the pretty curtains at the window, the baby in the pram, the husband as provider and protector and marriage as an end to the struggle towards maturity and personal identity.

These dreams seldom have a real person in the rôle of husband. He is just 'my husband'. There is no mud in the kitchen, no monotony, frustration or pain – all of which are part of real existence in marriage or outside it.

Just as the rose-coloured spectacles through which we have viewed the partner will inevitably come to be discarded, so will all the preconceptions about the married state. Slowly it comes to be seen, not as an end to growth, but as a beginning.

For it's really in our success or otherwise in relating to other people that we grow or fail to grow.

If the reality, therefore, becomes a problem: 'I didn't expect this'; 'He's not the man I married'; 'She's entirely changed since we married'; 'If this is marriage, I've had it ...', then the first step (leading to a lot more) is to ask the question: 'Is it that he's changed or is it that my dreams haven't?'

To realise that your expectations are still based on 'what could be' instead of 'what is' is not to say that you'll end up cynical and disillusioned – if you were that sort of person, you'd never have had dreams in the first place. And dreams are essential – they spur us on to attainable ideals, to creating love and tenderness, and reaching out to the world beyond the everyday.

But everyday life *is* nine parts 'everyday', and its roots are in what actually happens between two people with real feelings. Sooner or later we must come down to earth – and why not? The view may be lovely up there in the clouds, but down here life is possible – and potentially marvellous.

2 ... And the reality

Facing 'what is' is itself a problem for anyone who has kept themselves slightly out of touch with it, either by design or by compulsion.

There is the dependent, helpless sort of person who remains a 'child bride' and comes up with the problem that her husband is bossier than she realised. The reality is that she chose him because he was dominant and protecting and since she is, in fact, no longer a child, she resents what at first she sought out.

Frequently the reality of adjustment to someone else, however compatible and well-loved, looks pretty harsh to someone who has expected a kind of welding together of two people ('Two minds with but a single thought' or 'we're all in all to each other').

For a relationship implies just that – a relating to someone. It is not a joining, a sinking of one identity in another, a single unit. It is two separate, whole people facing each other, with a loving knowledge of each other, acceptance of their good and bad features, and, ultimately, a basic respect for the differences between them.

A true knowledge of someone else takes time, is painful sometimes, rewarding and exciting at others. To see them as they are and to accept what they are is love.

To look at love in this way is to remove a lot of the problems to do with reality. When you find something which does not tie up with the 'dreams of married bliss', then you will not feel cheated. On the contrary, you will come to see the dreams as cheating: 'This is real. This is how life is, how *he* is. This was something I didn't realise. Let's see how I can manage it. . . .' Give this a try.

Perhaps, at first, you cannot. You may find that, in spite of reality, you are still pulled by hopeless longings for things to be different, and by constant 'I wishes': 'I wish he were tidier'; 'I wish she wouldn't spend so much'; 'I wish I'd married her sister'; 'I wish I'd listened to mother'. Then it is probably time you had help towards wanting what you have rather than longing to have what you think you want. See Helping Agencies in Appendix A.

One thing about reality is that it can be altered. But, of course, you can't help to alter it if you won't accept it as real. If, for example, you still cling to the idea that satisfactory sex relations just happen along as a result of being in love, then this completely blocks you from realising that in your particular marriage they may not be too satisfying to either of you. So, of course, you can't begin to get down to the 'why' of it.

It might even prevent you from telling your husband how you feel about it – as if the problem might go away if you pretend it's not there. 'I wish he were a better lover or loved me more' takes the place of 'Why aren't things working out and how can we put them right?'. The dissatisfaction remains you. So you can't really begin to get down to the 'why' of it.

So the answer is that there is no married bliss for the asking. You make it, to put it simply, out of the real you and the real other person you married. Better find out what that is, don't you agree?

3 Surprises

In the past, surprises of the pleasant kind have been lauded as an essential part of happy marriage. 'Surprise her with a bunch of flowers', husbands were exhorted; 'cultivate an air of mystery', was the advice to wives. The assumption, presumably, was that people were a lot happier if they didn't know which way their partner was going to jump than if they did.

There was also the assumption that uncharacteristic moves by either the husband or wife somehow improved the relationship at a deeper level.

Yet it's clear, from anyone's experience of how people relate to each other and how they tick as individuals, that a bunch of flowers from a man who simply doesn't think of loving in terms of present-giving (and most married men don't) is not going to alter his way of thinking one bit, nor is it going to alter his wife's way of seeing him.

Nor will a wife's maddening Mona Lisa smile, when her husband asks her why she's smothered herself in perfume, do anything to make him think he's got a different woman in the marital bedroom from the same wife he's always had.

It's habit and consistency that cement people's real, secure feelings about each other, not surprises. But, of course, some people make a consistent habit of springing surprises and this can work very nicely.

All I'd say, then, is don't aim to surprise. It's a boomerang. The surprise that happens spontaneously is from *you*, not from someone else's idea of how you ought to be.

If the need to be surprised or to be surprising is something new and not a part of your nature or your partner's, then you can be pretty sure that your problem is Boredom (see point 82) or the feeling that you're taken for granted (point 81).

4 'We can't talk about anything'

This may mean that the partners simply don't talk to each other, except on practical matters. It might mean 'We can't talk about anything without arguing'.

Or it might mean that they do talk but that it isn't enough for one partner, or that the emotional atmosphere between them – whether of embarrassment, disapproval or resentment – paralyses their will towards 'talking out' anything except on the most superficial level.

In either case, if a husband and wife are not able to talk about what one or both partners would like to talk about, then there is what's called a breakdown in communication. The ability to communicate with anyone else about our feelings and views is such a variable quality that, in fact, real, lively communication between any two people is unfortunately pretty rare.

Most of us communicate with others rather patchily and at

a less than perfect level – we may have all the channels open and be able to 'talk' articulately and receive articulate responses but whether we get across to the other what we really mean and feel and whether they get across what they really mean and feel is a moot point.

In this sense we're all muddling along in the same boat and have learnt to accept the limitations of speech in everyday life.

But it's when the channels appear to be closed that there's a problem. This can range from the habit of letting things slip below the threshold of speech for the sake of peace or laziness or indifference – 'let sleeping dogs lie', 'least said, soonest mended' and all that – to the frightening stories one hears of couples living in the same house who haven't spoken a word to each other for twenty years.

When you don't seem to be talking about anything, and want to, then there are two answers at two different levels. One is the practical level – to use straightforward behaviouristic tactics, on the assumption that this is a bad habit to have got into and it should be broken.

The tactics are to talk. Just that. Choose your moment – not when he's just come home, but after a meal or a good TV play or on the way back from the local. Say 'I need to talk to you about this' and bust straight into the particular thing you wanted to talk about, ending with a question 'What do you feel about this? Are you as worried about this as I am?' so that he'll have to answer something.

A monologue is not communication, so beware of that. Don't expect problem-solving miracles out of it straight away – tho' in this sphere miracles can happen. The great thing is to open the lines and keep them open.

There is another level of non-communication, where it isn't just a habit, but represents a withdrawal from each other, or one from the other.

One or both may be experiencing such a degree of tension in the relationship that they are *unable* to communicate. Then the difficulty can be large – but not insuperable.

This can happen when there is anger or hurt on either side and, even more, when there are guilt-feelings. If, for example, a husband has been discovered in an act of infidelity, has told his wife everything, said he's sorry, and been forgiven, he will often want to 'stop talking about it'.

To the wife, however, the need to continue to 'chew over' for a while all the implications of what's happened and to get over the experience and truly know how it happened is still very much alive. She needs to communicate and he needs very much not to.

In circumstances like this, 'we can't talk about anything' usually means that he or she 'can't talk about that one thing' and it therefore blocks all communication, with the usually justified fear that the other will somehow get round to the topic that's obsessing him or her.

This happens, for instance, when there's a sex failure – he's impotent lately or she is always 'too tired' – and the one who can't manage it feels too guilty and inadequate to admit the trouble even exists.

Well, you've just got to be generous and brave about this. If your partner shows a need to chew something over, you can be certain of the fact that this is the only way he or she will get it in proportion. Block the chance of talk and you'll be landing yourself with a partner who's bitter, resentful and very likely humping an obsession round for the rest of her days. The worry you can't talk about is the dangerous one.

And if you're the one who needs to talk and just can't – either from guilt, shyness, anger or whatever – well, honestly I'm inclined to say that anything which helps to break down these inhibitions is a good thing – a stiff drink is a good aid – and then just leap in with both feet. (Again, choose your moment.)

'I'll burst if I don't get this off my chest' is a good opener. Or 'I badly need you to help me sort this out'. This is an appeal to be listened to which nobody of good faith and compassion can resist – even if he's temporarily your best enemy.

But never, never, when re-opening channels, start off with accusations, tears or a niggle of the 'when are you going to mend . . . ?' type (tho' that can and probably will come later).

The chances are that he's really just as anxious to thrash the matter out and will be relieved that you've taken over the burden of broaching the subject.

Once it *is* broached, then it's rather like having at last tackled the doctor about an embarrassing or highly personal complaint – once it's actually been turned into words, however awkwardly and incoherently, the whole problem miraculously loses its dead weight and gets moving in the direction of an answer.

And when that's been done – just keep the channels of communication open. This simply means saying how you feel about things instead of suffering or enjoying yourself in silence. This is far, far easier than re-opening channels which have been allowed to get blocked and unused.

5 'I can't call my soul my own'

If you feel you can't call your soul your own, it's either because you've actually let the family make more demands on your time, energy and emotions than you can reasonably tolerate, or you believe they're demanding more than they should from your private, 'free' self.

A husband whose wife checks his every move: 'When will you be back?; Who are you seeing?; Who was that girl who smiled at you in the butcher's?', might well say he can't call his soul his own. But he often virtually asks for this kind of possessive approach by being secretive about quite innocent arrangements and by being cruelly casual in the matter of household routine.

Many a husband has mistaken for jealousy and possessiveness the simple need of a woman to avoid an arduously-prepared meal ending up like a bit of dried leather. In matters of consideration, you can't entirely call your soul your own – it just has to be halved to co-exist.

Similarly, a woman who complains that the household job she's getting on with or the Sunday morning lie-in is continually interrupted by demands for this and that – 'Where are my socks?' 'Did you take that tie to the cleaners?'; 'What's for lunch?'; 'Where did you put the scissors?' and so on and so on – has clearly been a sight too anxious in the past to fetch, carry, put away, and generally tend the members of her family.

I know one woman who's shrieked at by husband and teenage children from whichever room in the house they happen to be. Does she shriek back that she's in the kitchen and that's where they'll find her if they want her? Not a bit – she drops everything and runs to find out what's wanted. 'I can't call my soul my own' she says.

But, of course, she's enjoying it and feels she's needed. She complains *with pride*. But her teenage boys are going to be proper tyrants and her husband already is – and she's a happy doormat. So just be sure that, when you reckon your soul's not your own, you didn't manoeuvre things around precisely that way.

But if you honestly feel robbed and pressured, then the only thing to do is to stand up for your own soul. 'I'm going to have a lie-down and if anyone disturbs me, except in a dire emergency, I'll be extremely angry.' They've been warned.

And, for him: 'I'm going down to the pub but as I might get drawn into a long session, let's eat first/have a cold bite/

I'll get something there/I'll bring back fish and chips/why don't you come too?'

Any of those alternatives is unlikely to make her feel you're an inconsiderate beast and retaliate with demand-noises. Your soul's your own and, moreover, you're a nice fellow.

6 'We're hardly even friendly'

This is a problem which depends entirely on what you think a friend should be. If, deep down, you reckon a friend is someone who always listens, always sympathizes, always boosts you up and always comes to your aid when it's needed, then you're probably someone who truly feels that you've never had a real friend at all and that you certainly haven't found one in your marriage partner.

So, as in so many other marriage problems, you need to make sure – before you label a partner as 'hardly even friendly' – that your expectations are not exceeding reality.

For, in truth, friendships are primarily relationships between equals – not between one who gives and one who gets – and as such they have their ups and downs and mixed feelings and tensions just as much as any other relationship.

The schoolgirl who says: 'She's my best friend and I hate her' is putting into a nut-shell the mixture of feelings we all have about anyone who's close to us and in whom we invest any deep feelings at all.

The first answer then, is to ponder on whether you are not perhaps expecting too much sweetness and light, too much agreement and blandness from the 'friendship' part of your marriage.

Perhaps, what you see as ill-will, grumpiness or refusal to talk things over when you feel like it, is not an unfriendly reaction to you at all, or, indeed, any reaction to *you*.

It might be a reaction to something which is going on inside the partner – to do with health, work, friends, or the way life's going – and he or she simply cannot pull out the comfort, sympathy or friendly behaviour you are asking for yourself.

Which brings me to the second possible avenue to a solution; to have a friend, you have to *be* one. You have to be prepared to be leant against as well as to lean on. This is one of those obvious things which are so often overlooked because they *are* so obvious.

Clearly you simply don't get the bright 'Hello's' and 'What sort of day have you had?' if you don't offer this kind of friendliness yourself. And you are likely to get a withdrawal from easy, casual friendly relations if you can't accept the odd: 'Oh, do shut up about that' as well as dish it out yourself.

7 'He never takes me out'

Wives who do not go out with their husbands in the evenings are rather apt to put it this way: 'He never *takes* me out', thus providing a clue to why they don't go out together.

So often, you see, the wish to have a social life together masks the wish to be asked out, to be given a treat, to be courted, far more than the actual wish to share as partners an evening's entertainment.

As in a number of other things about marriage, going out together is largely a matter of habit and accepted responses. Before the children come, going out is easy and if a wife finds then that she's left by herself at home a lot, then it's likely she's married someone who likes to take his pleasures separately.

The best thing she can do in that case, apart from the time-honoured moves for encouraging the man to want to have her along, is to take her pleasures separately too.

There's absolutely nothing conducive to marriage-breakdown about a husband going off to the pub and his wife to an evening class on the same evening, if they agree to it. In fact it could lead to an enrichment of the times they *are* together.

But when the children are young, there is inevitably a period when the wife is more tied to the home, more tired, less inclined to dress up and face the outside world. The effort to find a sitter-in, alter your hem-length, get the evening chores done in double-quick time, and settle the kids, often daunts a mother who would quite like to go out and would benefit from it if she did.

Often a habit is formed whereby she doesn't go out, even when there's a good opportunity. In time this can turn into a slightly martyred feeling which becomes a comfortable fit (see point 79).

So you get those familiar occasions when the wife, secretly daunted by the prospect of going out, turns down her husband's suggestions with all sorts of excuses: 'How can I – with all this ironing?'; 'I was going to wash my hair!'; 'If old Tom's going to be there, I couldn't face it'; 'I can't ask Mum to sit-in – she just lets the kids go wild . . .'

So he stops asking. Or just accepts that she doesn't want to go out. And perhaps she really doesn't. But she still wants to be *asked*. She still wants her arm twisted or everything laid on.

So if you honestly do want to go out with him, you've really got to make it an equal pleasure – it's got to be something of a treat for him too, after all, rather than a duty to satisfy a need of yours.

There's a film on he might like, so you suggest you both go. (Next time it could be a film you'd like.) If there's a party, an invitation to eat or something, don't say: 'Will you take me' – say 'Shall we go?'.

You aim at switching the whole thing round from the neglected 'little woman' wanting to be urged into enjoying herself into the grown woman who'll be a good companion for an evening's shared pleasure.

If taking you out is seen by your husband as a necessary chore which you demand from him, you may load him with enough guilt to haul you off for a drink now and again but, honestly, is it going to be fun for either of you?

8 Housewife's blues

This is a pretty broad term to cover all those feelings of unease and dissatisfaction covered by the phrases 'the captive mother', 'prisoner at the sink', 'graduates with dish-pan hands' and any others you happen to know and I don't.

There's no doubt that not every woman – or perhaps *no* woman – finds absolute fulfilment in the frequently monotonous, repetitive business of running a home and family.

She may find sufficient fulfilment in bits of it but there will inevitably be times when she thinks: 'Is this all I'm *for* – washing this plate for the hundredth time, mopping up the kitten's puddle, telling the story about the green bear?'.

The world shrinks. She loses sight of distant goals, and life becomes a pattern of tiny, negative achievements – 'Thank heaven the cake didn't burn today' – with tiny rewards and tiny setbacks.

Often the setbacks – if they are repeated often enough (and the door-handle which won't work properly, the dripping-tap, the faulty gadget all come into this category) grow from tiny into enormous. And it's possible to find that daily life becomes a constant inner battle against frustration and disorder.

The inner battle often takes the form of resentment at the husband, or, more likely, the blues, – a deadened response to the good things, merging, in particularly anxious or frustrated people, into real depression.

If there is depression – which is not simply unhappiness, but is characterised by crying jags, a 'nothing matters' feeling, a failure of response and a kind of despair – then a doctor's help is essential.

But most often the blues don't reach this stage because most of us are sensible enough to do something about these blues before they escalate.

What to do? Well a wife can do either of two fundamental things:

1 She can accept that there will be 'blue' times. This is part of life – for a man too – and all she needs to do is to *know* that it will pass.

Meanwhile there's no reason why she shouldn't indulge herself during a blues – break up the routine a bit, let the floor stay unpolished, take the children to the park. Clocks are not nearly the tyrants we make them out to be – we can do so much to alter the quality of the hour, even if we can't alter its quantity.

2 She can *say* she feels as she does, instead of bottling up the resentment. She can have a good moan to her husband, first explaining that that is *all* she is doing. She's not, she may need to say, blaming him, expecting things to be altered or feeling all that self-pitying – she just needs to moan.

The husband, for his part, can let her. It's no skin off his nose and unless he's very short on confidence, he should be able to accept her gripes as well as she, we hope, accepts his moans about the boss, the garage, etc.

See also in Appendix A under Housewives Register for another possible remedy for the blues.

9 Sharing the work-load

This is a big source of problems. The basic difficulty is that the boundary-lines between the wife's duties and the husband's duties have become so fuzzy that we can hardly distinguish them at all.

If a wife is earning, and is jointly responsible with the husband for maintaining the family, should he or shouldn't he share her responsibility for running the home? If she does the washing-up, ought he to do the drying? Who gets the fuel in? Who ought to make the early morning tea?

You could go on like this for ever, wondering about 'shoulds' and 'oughts', and getting nowhere. For what has happened, in the absence of fixed rules and unalterable duties, is that it rests now with every individual husband and wife to sort out their own working arrangements, in a way that suits their needs and their marriage.

So I should scrap all your notions about what's manly and what's womanly if I were you. And about what other people will think if it's known that you can change a nappy expertly and your wife is a dab-hand under the car-bonnet. If this works out and you're both happy about it, that's all that matters.

But, of course, there can be conflicts between you about who does what. Perhaps you wouldn't iron your own shirts, in a million years, and it's your wife's most hated chore – so who irons the shirts?

Well, at the bottom of every conflict like this are your feelings about it. For where there's a question of choice and preference and 'what my mother used to do' and 'the way things were done in *my* family', we get emotionally worked up about these little matters.

So that, in the end, it's desperately important for the husband not so much to have his shirts ironed as to feel he has the kind of wife who will iron them.

She, on the other hand, not so much just can't face ironing a shirt as doesn't want to see herself as the kind of wife who performs ritual tasks for her husband ('Just his slave'). Ultimately it looks, to him, as if she's not ironing his shirts because she doesn't love him. And, in her eyes, he's wanting her to iron them because *he* doesn't love her.

Apply this example to any chore or responsibility you've been arguing about recently and you'll be surprised to see just how much emotion you've invested in it and how far away you've moved from the simple necessity for getting the job done somehow, with not much importance attached to who does it.

Try to prune it of all these emotions. Get rid of the idea that there's a competition on to prove you're always on the go and the other is just an idler. You both work hard and you know it – to run a home and family well you both *have* to.

If neither of you likes ironing shirts, there are drip-dry ones and there's the laundry or you can do half on Monday and he can do the rest on Thursday.

One good thing about being on the same side in this matter – the two of you against the heap of responsibilities and chores – is that together you'll be much more enthusiastic about whittling them down to what's really necessary, or farming them out to a paid service.

The question then becomes not: 'Should I help with the

washing-up or can I engineer it so that she does it all but I don't feel guilty about it?' but instead: 'Can we afford a washing-up machine?'.

If you both hate washing-up, you'll find you can afford it all right.

10 Separate interests

If a man or woman has any interests at all, apart from the family and home, they are bound to have some interests different from those of their partner.

And why not? They are different people. However close we want to be emotionally to another person, there is no possible way of making them have the same enthusiasms, same likes and dislikes or the same thoughts as we have. Yet, what a lot of time husbands and wives waste trying to do just that!

Mostly the wives, I'm afraid – for some women do tend to live their lives through the men they love. They feel 'left out' and almost abandoned if the husband likes something they do not.

'His one passion is fishing – he goes off every week-end and leaves me at home. I can't find any interest in it but he won't see my point of view'. What I want to ask is: 'And what are *you* interested in? Or could it be that you've no room for anything except the absorbing interest of resenting his?'.

If interests genuinely coincide – that's fine. But this is not something which *ought* to happen just because two people have joined up in one major interest – living together, loving each other and raising a family.

There are parts of each that this interest does not use, and these have to be satisfied outside the relationship. And they *can* be met without taking anything from the relationship.

It seems to me that it is only when a partner has failed to see the other as a separate person, with his or her own interests and enthusiasms, and has wanted him to merge with her, that he's likely to cultivate more and more separate interests as an escape from this form of possessiveness.

Golf-clubs, pubs and societies of all kinds contain a pretty large proportion of men who are simply there 'to get away from their wives', to establish their separateness, their right to a mind of their own and to escape the very nasty feeling that someone is wanting you to be a different person from what you are.

On the other hand, those husbands and wives who have not, from the start, expected to offer up their entire selves to merging with the partner have limited the area of their 'together-ness'. But the nature of their relationship in that particular area is just what marriage can be – two separate, whole people, with all their fascinating differences, alongside each other emotionally.

So there is no 'should' or 'should not' about separate inter-ests. They are there and have to be given room to flourish. That goes for a wife too – be glad that she wants to go and learn Italian on her own (and cook your own supper).

If you can't accept these separate interests but try to kill them or make the other feel guilty for having them, then sure as eggs you are driving yourselves into more separateness and apartness than you ever dreamed of. You know the saying: 'The looser the knot, the tighter the bonds'.

11 Hospitality

Most married couples enjoy having friends in. If you don't, then that's the way you are and I don't suppose you have any problems about it (or get asked to other peoples' homes either).

If one partner does and the other doesn't, then it's likely that things will fall out the wife's way since it's extremely diffi-cult for a husband to bring people into the home or keep them out of it if his wife is not co-operating (see point 43).

If you're not happy about the amount or the kind of enter-taining you do at home, then the first obvious step is to find out why your partner is either holding back or overdoing it.

'The expense of it' is often produced as an excuse, but this is invariably a rationalisation unless you actually are on the bread-line. People who enjoy having friends in but live on the smell of an oil-rag still *do* have people in. If friendship is the true basis of these encounters, it really doesn't matter if they're only offered a glass of cider. (If they know you well, they'll have the sense to eat first.)

Apart from hermit-like tendencies in a partner – which simply have to be accepted, since there are people who do not need or want much contact with their fellows – the usual underlying reason for a reluctance to have people in is a feeling of inadequacy about some aspect of the whole thing.

A wife with little self-confidence may perpetually feel that her home is too shabby, her cooking too bad, her social man-ner too awkward to be put on display.

Reassurance is the only answer to this ... not the kind that tries to convince her that her home is actually a model one, but of the kind that points out how little this matters beside what she *can* offer friends. (Everyone has got something – dig it out.)

In the same way, an ambitious husband may feel that his home isn't good enough, his style of life not impressive enough or even that his wife isn't sophisticated enough to risk having in people he wants to impress.

Unfortunately, a very ambitious man, who is as unsure as this, will want to impress *everyone*, even friends he doesn't need to impress, and this *is* rather a tricky problem.

Perhaps the only answer here is to bide your time until he's made his setting suitably impressive (as he undoubtedly will), and meanwhile he'd probably be happy to entertain people in a restaurant or club instead (which spares you a lot of trouble anyway).

The wife who's too hospitable for the husband's comfort or pocket clearly has a basic problem about not liking to be alone with herself, or with him. She's got to keep on dishing out hospitality in order to feel she's of any importance and to have people around to establish that she exists at all.

If this hasn't reached the stage when all the spongers in the neighbourhood are whooping it up every night in your sitting-room (in which case she needs help and a marriage counsellor would be the person to get it from initially) the best answer is to do your best to make her feel somebody when she's *not* dishing out hospitality, i.e. praise, encourage and love the grown-up things in her. If she's all child and 'little girl lost', then you'll need to consider that perhaps this is why you married her and that you might as well accept and join in what goes with it.

If it's your husband who brings people in more than you like or can cope with, the only answer is *not* to cope every single time. So long as you always rally round with drinks and eats he'll naturally expand his 'hosting' to the bitter limit.

Fix one night first as 'not at home' – you're going to wash your hair, cut a dress out on the sitting-room floor or go round to Joan's place. He may still see his friends, but elsewhere.

All you need to be sure of is that this is what you want. Yours is the choice between having his conviviality under your roof and under your eye or having it take place somewhere else. You won't change him into a slippers-by-the-fire man, that's for certain.

12 Irritating habits

Don't let this discourage you but a habit is a habit and *you* can do nothing to break someone else's. If he sucks his soup noisily, has a laugh that grates, blows his nose like a trumpet, scratches himself or jingles his money in his pocket, the most you can do is draw his attention to it *once*.

If he didn't know he had the habit, this will enlighten him. But it won't necessarily make him want to stop and he might not be able to even if he wants to.

The same goes for her sniffing, letting ash drop down her front, beginning every conversation with 'I must say' or picking at her nail-varnish.

Habits of this order are not consciously willed and cannot be willed undone. One could say that they *happen* rather than that they are actions, and therefore one could not hope to make them not happen except by bringing about some alteration in their source.

But the source is the personality of the person with the habit. The noisy soup-sucker, one could say, is more intent on getting fed than on the manner of his feeding; the grating laugh comes from uncertainty or shyness (or did when it first became a habit); the sniffing comes from being too busy (or feeling too busy) to fetch a handkerchief – and so on.

So, unless you're hell-bent on altering the kind of person your partner is (point 40) you can only tackle the irritating habits at the receiving end, i.e. by ceasing to be irritated by them. Being irritated by them is not a habit – it's under your control.

If you have even a bit of insight into why they happen and the nervous springs at their source, you can understand and accept them instead of condemning them. (Funnily enough, habits are about the only things about which you can truly say that, if you don't look at them, they often go away.)

If you're poised to strike at every sniff or laugh, the result will probably be a nervous redoubling of the activity. If you register it's there but can take it, the source of the habit may well dry up and your help could be welcome: 'If you just let me know when I'm doing it, I'll be able to check it'.

Above all, the way not to be irritated is to get out of your mind the idea that every sniff or laugh or trumpet-blow is *designed* to annoy you. It's fatally easy to fall into the way of thinking that *because* it irritates that's its whole purpose in life. This is all part of the not-being-separate idea which I talked about in point 10.

The habit is involuntary, rests entirely in the other person and is not sent to try you. The sooner you can live with it, the sooner the other person will be able to live without it.

13 'We never have a holiday'

Perhaps some families really are too hard-up to have a holiday. But since you can actually have a holiday for the same amount of money you would have spent at home if you'd been there (I know because I've done it), we do have to face the fact that any husband and wife who feels resentful at the lack of a break of some kind either doesn't really want one or is being a bit inflexible about the kind of holiday she's willing to call a holiday.

When we think of a holiday we do tend to think of the *perfect* holiday. A week with friends doesn't count because you know the place and people too well; camping doesn't count because you have to wash up and do the cooking just the same (only it isn't the same – that's the point); a rented cottage doesn't count because you have to do a bit of housework; and, for him, a seaside hotel doesn't count because he couldn't fish, or watch cricket or play golf or whatever.

So you have to be pretty careful that you're not limiting your idea of a 'real' holiday to the 'dream' holiday, and that you haven't been holding out for a perfect fortnight where you don't have to lift a finger, the sun shines all day and your husband's so attentive to you that it's like a second honeymoon.

If you are thinking along these lines, you certainly can say you never have a holiday and, by the same count, nor does anyone else.

So one answer is to lower your sights a bit. Another answer, if there's never even been any question of having a holiday of any kind, is to ask yourself why not.

Holidays don't just happen. You *take* a holiday. Someone has to get weaving early in the year on combing the ads, getting brochures, working out costs, saving the money, booking this and that. There's a lot to it, even on the cheapest sort of holiday there is and if one of you doesn't stir your stumps you can sit until August longing for a holiday and then wonder why you're not having one.

The third answer, if you happen to have a partner who just doesn't believe in holidays, is to take one for yourself. There's no lack of loyalty or breaking of the marriage vows in husbands and wives being apart for a week or so.

Husbands can and do manage this in the interests of work (or pleasure). For a woman it takes a bit more planning and management (especially if the kids are still young) but it can be done – if you want to.

I say 'if you want to' because some wives are basically reluctant to take a break. They reckon they're indispensable (and don't much want to discover they're not) or they have genuine anxieties about leaving home and family.

But if you have these kinds of anxieties – what might happen while you're not there – then you really do need a holiday, both for your health's sake and to find out how baseless the anxieties are.

part ii Feelings

Elsewhere in this book, but particularly in this Part, I've said so much about the feelings marriage partners have about themselves and about their partners, that this seems a good place to explain why they are emphasized so much.

There is some explanation for this in the Introduction. But you might still think that feelings aren't nearly so vital to a marriage as what actually happens in fact.

If a husband loses his job, for example, that's a practical fact which brings marriage problems in its wake for sure. What have feelings really got to do with it?

What does it matter what the partners' feelings are when the plain fact is that there's less money coming into the home, the husband is around the house all day or searching for a job and both are wondering how on earth they're going to manage?

And that's an unhappy marriage, isn't it? And won't it be a happy one again when he does get a job? So why bother about feelings?

Well, think of the variety of ways this crisis is faced, according to the feelings of the partners. If the husband has little confidence in himself, he'll feel a bit despairing about getting another job. He'll need his wife to feel supportive and hopeful and show it.

But if his wife shares this no-confidence in him – and has perhaps unwittingly contributed to it – she'll feel despairing too and pull him down further – 'you'll never get another job the way you're going on. . . .' Or the wife may have basic feelings of insecurity, so that this crisis throws her into a panic and her only way out is to shower her husband with her anxieties – 'what happens if this goes on for another month, have you thought of that? How are we going to manage the HP? Why didn't you take that garage job? You can't afford to be choosy. . . .'

Another wife, who has a basic trust in herself and in others, will face the difficulties calmly, cope with her side of the problem and support him in his side of the problem.

For any couple, loss of earnings *is* a problem. But you can see that the feelings each partner brings to it can make all the difference between a shared problem, solved by efforts at practical solution, or a snowball which gathers to it all sorts of other problems to do with feelings.

This Part, therefore, is about the feelings which each of us brings to bear on the marriage relationship as a whole, on the way we view the partner and on the ways we cope with problems.

14 The longing for love

One of the trickiest things about love is that it's not what you actually receive in the way of love which makes you feel loved or not, but how lovable you feel you are.

For example, there's the woman who puzzles (and often irritates) her husband by continually asking: 'Do you really love me? Tell me you love me. I know you married me, but that could have been for other reasons. Do *really* love me?'.

At least she can voice her uncertainties about being lovable. Far unhappier is the woman who has these uncertainties but can only express them in fierce competitiveness in work or in the home, or in an over-all feeling of inferiority and inadequacy.

A major motive for infidelity in either sex is invariably a bid to gain this 'loved feeling' by a man or woman who has never felt lovable, or not lovable enough for his or her own expectations.

This is a big subject and needs a lot more delving into if your problem seems to be: 'He doesn't love me'. There are suggestions for reading-matter on this subject in Appendix B.

But it will meanwhile help to recognise that the longing to be loved is basic to everyone. It is not, however, an unrealistic longing – to be loved all the time, reassured constantly and well-nigh worshipped – for anyone who has had an experience of feeling loved in an accepting, realistic way in the past (by parents, or by parent-substitutes, in adolescence or in adult life).

A man or woman who has had this experience cannot lose it and subsequently will have this basic lovable feeling revived in the day-to-day relationship with the marriage partner.

It is confirmed by his being there, his very choice of her as a wife, the small things he attends to for the family's sake. It is not put in hazard by the things he doesn't do or his failure to remember her birthday or to say: 'I love you'.

Other people, however, who have not had the experience of feeling loved (which may have nothing to do with whether they were actually loved or not) cannot recognise love when it's offered,

It's as if their receiving apparatus was at fault. They are only tuned to receive physical or obvious manifestations of love (hence compulsive love-affairs, a desire for presents, admiration and constant 'proof' of love).

If your partner is of this kind, what's the answer?

After what I've said you hardly need me to add that all you can do is to continue to love and show it.

And I mean love in the widest sense – not necessarily giving the excessive approval he or she is demanding, but the consistent, understanding acceptance that will help him or her to grow up into the ability to receive love (to feel lovable) and therefore to give it. A tall order? It certainly is. But then so is marriage.

15 The flight of magic

This often seems like an end of love, when the magic goes. But it's really the stage of passing from 'being in love' to 'loving'.

Problems seem to arise when a one or both partners have thought that these two things 'being in love' and 'loving' are the same thing, or b they have recognised the difference but have thought that the 'loving' part is also something that just happens to you, and follows as a matter of course on the excitement and magic of the other.

This transition is usually presented as: 'I just don't love him anymore'; 'I don't feel the same about her'; 'I thought I loved him, but I don't'; 'I know now that I married the wrong person'.

Now no-one can think like this unless they have been, as it were, waiting on deep love, passively expecting the relationship to develop of its own accord into that mutual acceptance and understanding that most people mean by 'loving'.

Or perhaps they have passively waited for the magic to live on and felt it as a cruel blow of fate that it fled in the face of day-to-day life with the beloved.

Well, as we know, being in love has a lot to do with idealization and finding in the other person the qualities we most need to find.

There is usually just enough resemblance to our ideal in the person we fall in love with – it may be only the colour of eyes or the fact that he's witty – for us to pin on to him the job lot of our longings, dreams and needs.

This accounts for the rose-coloured spectacles of love when beauty, good looks, strength, wisdom – everything we most want to see in another – are assuredly in the eye of the beholder.

And when the rose-coloured spectacles are discarded – or, more likely, wrenched off by the demands of reality – then it marks the difference between the grown-up and the child as to whether or not we can start adjusting to a real relationship with a real person who has faults, weaknesses, and irritating traits like everyone else.

It is never that love has flown, always that there has been no attempt to create it out of that small, powerful seed which brought the partners into involvement with each other in the first place.

This needs a lot of effort and adjustment. It requires an initial commitment, when you are still 'in love', to the idea that continuing to love someone is a matter of choice, not of fate. When you marry, you 'promise to love' – a promise which seems ridiculous to people who believe that: 'You can't help it, if you don't love someone anymore'.

But we all can; we have to accept the burden, or the joy – depending on how you look at it – of our individual responsibility for our own feelings and actions.

We love where we mean to love. Commitment is at the heart of this. Rather than thinking: 'I will marry this man because I love him' we should really think: 'I will love this man because I am going to marry him, or because I am married to him'.

What follows from this *will* to love is the acceptance of all the things you don't like about him, when the spectacles are gone. There is no perfect partner; the magic would wear off with anyone, but you can recreate it where you sincerely choose to love.

So if you feel that: 'I don't love him/her anymore', I can only say: 'Then you never have loved him/her at all – you have only been in love and that has ended'.

And if things look so bleak that you can't even begin to see how to start the real loving, then perhaps you are one of those unlucky people who don't quite know what loving is, and have never, in your whole life, had the experience of loving and being loved (see point 37).

If that's so, you'd be wise to talk it all over with a marriage guidance counsellor or someone else.

Then maybe you'll find that your only difficulty is in not recognising your own loving feelings and those of your partner. What you thought was a loss of love on both sides could be merely a change in its nature.

Most of us do not like to feel that we can hate as well as love and that the hate is invariably felt towards people we also love. But we vaguely acknowledge this when we talk about 'love/hate relationships'.

Perhaps among our friends we occasionally recognise that a particular relationship, between husband and wife, father and son, mother and daughter, is one that veers between strong loving feelings and others, just as strong, of hostility or resentment.

But in truth all relationships which contain any feelings at all include these two sides of the same coin. A child, if it loves its mother when she satisfies him, will equally hate her when she doesn't. It is only when there is little or no feeling for her at all – as in an autistic child – that there will be no hate, nor any love either. There is only seeming indifference.

Similarly, when we as adults love someone very much and are dependent on them for love and satisfactions in return, we bring into that love – if it is truly a feeling one – all the range of our emotions, including fear and hostility.

It's often been said that the opposite of love is not hate, but indifference. This ought to be engraved on marriage lines or something and then maybe a lot more marriage partners would feel free to accept the hostile part of their feelings and accept the partner's hostile feelings too.

If you know that where there's love there's hate you can allow the hate to find expression without taking it as a sign of being unloved – for that's what being hurt really is.

But, on the whole, women are more prone to suppress their hostility than men. It seems more difficult for them to say: 'Look, you've really made me angry by doing that and I'm going to have it out with you' which is an honest, constructive way of dealing with a moment of hostility.

Instead they tend to think it more feminine, or just more in line with their image of themselves, to bottle it all up, sit in meaningful silence throwing murderous looks at him, or go out and tick the kids off on some trumped-up excuse.

Another favourite way is to bang the saucepans or kick the cat or, even worse, keep a switched-off air of martyrdom and mystery about the home for a few days. The hostility there is patently evident but there'd only be half a problem or no problem at all if she'd put it where it belongs, in the relationship with her partner.

This isn't to say that hostile feelings shouldn't be controlled.

It is obviously no part of grown-up married life for the partners to regress to the kind of free expression of rage and hate one allows to disturbed children.

But the point is that if the hostility just isn't recognised, it can't be controlled very well. Admittedly, it finds channels other than free verbal or physical expression but these ways are not seen as expressions of hostility at all. They are rationalized.

You drive the car exceptionally fast because you're late. You bang the saucepans because you're in a hurry. You kick the cat because it got in your way. You tick young Peter off because he didn't clean his shoes before bed-time (although he never does) and so on. Never because you are just feeling angry!

So the hostility spreads itself around and can easily end in the nagging, complaining kind of person whose anger is spread thin over her whole life and leaves little room for love (see also point 18).

This is not control, and it can't be when the hostility isn't even seen to exist. But once you can see that hostile feelings towards a loved person are there, and are real feelings, then you have some choice about whether or not they are to be expressed and how.

In the light of this, one straightforward admission: 'I'm angry with you' could be a more loving and certainly more constructive thing to do than a million bitter words bitten back or a host of resentful silences.

17 The urge to dominate

If you have something of an urge to dominate, it's pretty unlikely you know about it yourself (this is one of those traits in ourselves we don't care to know about).

But your partner will know about it all right, and it's certain that you can recognise it in other people: 'She wears the trousers in that family'; 'He's got her right under his thumb'; 'She's just a door-mat'; 'He's hen-pecked'. And so on.

These are familiar pictures, to an outsider, of marriages in which one partner has taken a dominant role. And, for all that, they may not be unhappy or 'bad' marriages – both partners may be perfectly comfortable in the roles they've taken on, whether the one on top or the one underneath, in spite of the token protests they might make about 'having to manage everything myself' or 'not being able to call my soul my own'.

Where there do seem to be problems is when both partners feel an underlying, vital compulsion to engage in a battle of wills, to score points, to come out on top, have the last word, be the one who controls the relationship.

For people like this – who are unable to relax, let things take their course and let the other person be – it really does feel unsafe and threatening to lose an argument or not get your own way about quite trivial things – like having the teapot kept on the right of the stove instead of the left.

This is something you need to understand if you have a partner who's inclined to be bossy, or if you're bossy yourself – that it invariably comes from a deep fear of being overwhelmed by life and people if you don't do everything possible to manipulate them *your* way.

When you're dealing with someone who wants to dominate and control, therefore, you're really dealing with someone who's frightened. This is perhaps something you can help yourself with, if you perceive that a battle of wills is going on and that you're heavily engaged yourself and *must win*.

Simply try giving way for a change. Be brave about this. Do it once and you'll discover that letting go and appearing to lose often turns you both into winners.

Reckon calmly and cold-bloodedly on how much it actually matters if a meal's served late, he leaves his socks on the floor or he puts off a mending-job until next week. The sky won't fall. Life will go on – there's absolutely no-one pushing you but yourself.

If he's insisting that something is done now which could be left till later (and you don't want to do it now anyway), what's the point of getting up steam and yelling back: 'I'm jolly well not going to do it just when you want me to. I'll do it in my own good time'?

You can equally accept this as *not* an attack on you – which it isn't, but an anxiety in *him* – and tell him reasonably: 'Yes, of course, I know you're worried about it. I'm going to do it this evening when I'll have the time.'

18 Nagging

Nagging is another aspect of the urge to dominate and control (point 17). It's not just a feminine trait either. Husbands appear to go in for nagging too, if by nagging we mean the constant reminders by one partner of an omission or failure by the other.

The first point about this is – are you absolutely certain

that the nagging is coming from another person and not from inside you?

Yes, I know the feeling of being nagged is unmistakable, and that someone who's nagged has no doubts at all about being nagged, but what he or she often doesn't recognise clearly is where the nagging is coming *from*.

Often, you see, someone who's pretty hard on themselves, and tends to have a nagging conscience, suffers from continuous thoughts along the lines of: 'I really must get that done. It's very wrong of me to leave that so long. And when I've dealt with that, I really ought to get onto such-and-such. Am I really managing all right? I wish I didn't feel so hustled! I haven't really the time for all these things. Why do people expect so much of me? It would be all right if there weren't all this pressure to get on with things . . .'.

'All this pressure' is readily switched from its source inside him to a source outside. That's the way the human mind works. So that, if his wife so much as uses the can-opener she's asked him to fix, remarking: 'I wish this blessed thing would work properly', his nagging conscience swings into attack, disguised as an attack by *her*, and he leaps to his own defence with: 'I wish you'd stop nagging about it. I've told you I'll do it when I've got a moment'.

So that's one answer to nagging – make sure it's not that you have a nagger inside you. If you have, well you're the only person who's capable of keeping it in order, either by relaxing the standards it demands of you, or actually doing some of the things it's driving you to do, instead of worrying so much about how and when to do them.

Another answer to nagging is to look past the actual content of the nagging (which is often quite irrelevant) and ask yourself why your partner needs to nag at all.

Is he or she lonely, perhaps? Could she be feeling neglected and 'left out' and this is her way of hauling you in? Is she in a state of tension, unable to let things be? Most of these things can be answered by your consideration and understanding, by getting at what's nagging *her*.

It could also be a physical problem – better note if the nagging takes place for a couple of days regularly once a month. Nagging, or what looks like nagging, is often an expression of pre-menstrual tension and this is something which can be treated medically. It's a sure thing that if this is her problem she feels just as unhappy and nagged by it as you do. Despite the outward signs, no-one actually *enjoys* nagging. So encourage her to see the doctor.

19 In the dog-house

This is the feeling of 'being always in the wrong'. Most of us are so precariously balanced between feeling 'I'm an O.K. person' and 'I'm no good' that it's really quite easy for someone we love and live with to confirm one feeling or the other by their response to us.

With consistent love and support flowing between a husband and wife – notwithstanding the rows and resentments they have in the ordinary ups and downs of life – both of them can have an almost continuous and infinite feeling of being 'OK' people – basically good and loving and loved.

If, on the other hand, the 'I'm no good' feeling is the one that's getting constant confirmation in all sorts of little ways – picking at each other, knocking her achievements or crowing about his failures, hurtful comparisons and so on – then it's easy to absorb a permanent feeling of being in the wrong, and no good, and unable to do anything right.

The beginning of an answer to the problem – and it is only a beginning – is to seize this important point: that nobody is either 'all wrong' or, for that matter, 'all right'.

Like everyone else, you are full of right bits, wrong bits, good bits, bad bits. Nobody, but *nobody,* not even the person you love best in the world, can cause you to be any different. All she or he can do is to confirm the feelings about yourself that you already have, either the good feelings in preponderance, or the bad, or, in truly mature, clear-eyed relationships, both sorts of feelings.

So the chances are that if you do feel that you're always in the wrong, this is a feeling you tend to have about yourself in any case, no matter how other people are reacting to you.

What you need most, therefore, is to get a more balanced, truer picture of yourself. How you do this is up to you – we all have our individual ways of re-discovering self-confidence, some by religion, some by mixing more with other people, some by helping others, some by psychotherapy, some by work or studies or hobbies.

Another answer is this: if you *are* being picked on, criticised and found wanting in spite of the fact that you are not 'all wrong' – since nobody is – then the obvious inference is that the person who's doing the knocking and belittling is being driven by some problems of her own or his own. It might be helpful to find out together what those problems are.

Quarrels are very much an outcome of feelings, but they are seldom feelings which have anything to do with what you're quarrelling about.

You probably find that most of your quarrels begin on the same topic – money, mother-in-law, sex, and end on the same note – either impasse, tears, slamming doors or kiss and make up, according to your natures.

Or else the pattern is that you quarrel about almost everything you set out to 'discuss'.

Because quarrels are, in the main, an outlet for feelings which need to find expression and which can and do find expression in far more harmful ways if quarrels are taboo, I find it rather difficult to think of quarrels as problems in themselves.

But there are problems attached to them. Couples wonder if they do lasting damage when, for example, hurtful things are said. Or they wonder if they little by little nibble bits out of a basically loving relationship and kill love. What about quarrels in front of the children? Is this bad? What about quarrels in public?

Well, the way I see it is this: quarrelling is a natural accompaniment to having an alive, feeling relationship with someone (see point 16). If you feel anything for someone, then you feel anger, spitefulness, and jealousy towards them sometimes as well as love, desire and affection at others (or even all of those at the same time!)

But, like some other aspects of any close relationship, such as caressing, or the exchange of confidences, quarrelling is a rather private and personal business. It's something which takes place between the personal, emotional areas of a man and woman. In a word, quarrelling is intimate.

So, like kissing or memory-raking, I rather think quarrels should not take place in public. Whether you conduct them when the children can hear or see is up to you. It depends on how far you think they are capable of viewing the intimacies of adult relationships without becoming insecure or frightened by them.

If the quarrels are very bitter, and if the children are not also around when you make up, then they might be alarmed at the ill-feeling displayed and fear that it might be permanent.

On this score, it's clearly better that they know of several quarrels and observe the *status quo* which *always* follows them than get embroiled in just one.

So, if you're inveterate quarrellers, it would seem better not to go to great lengths to keep them out of hearing of the children – which is impossible anyway in most houses. But if you rarely quarrel except for one flaming row annually, then I should make sure they don't know about it.

21 Loss of temper

If you're on the receiving end of physical violence, then the only immediate answer is to tell someone else about it. If the violent partner can't control it by himself, you certainly can't.

A Probation Officer will always help with this kind of marital problem. Or you could tell your doctor about it. Calling the police in when there's an emergency helps to 'keep the peace' temporarily, but can't of course do anything to help the underlying problem.

If your husband or wife suffers from flare-ups that are verbally very nasty but not physically damaging, it can, of course, be just as unnerving for you. Whether he or she is anxious to control these outbursts or, more usually, is very contrite in between and tries to control them, the answer is the same – that he or she needs help.

Your doctor will either help, if you or your partner tells him about the difficulty, or put you on to someone who can. A marriage guidance counsellor will also help whichever one of you (if not both) cares to make the first approach with this problem.

Lastly, there is the partner who's short-tempered for periods at a time ('he's like a bear with a sore head') or loses his temper occasionally on one particular issue or in similar situations.

This is probably his particular way of dealing with frustrations or feelings of inadequacy – we all have our own ways. Like feelings of hostility, these dissatisfactions have to have some outlet.

A partner can either accept these outlets, and make sure they're harmless by not over-reacting with attitudes of hurt or indignation or governessy 'you ought to control yourself' type of remarks; or, more lovingly, observe what prompts them and attempt to understand just what frustrations and dissatisfactions are at the bottom of them.

One consolation – of all the 'funny little ways' we come to accept and modify in a partner, loss of temper is really one of the less difficult ones. It's at least open and straightforward. Someone who's in a bad temper and is able to lose it, in speech or action, is a much better bet than the man or woman who has to hold onto it, and spread it round thinly under a cover of icy good-will (see point 16).

22 That unwanted feeling

'He'd rather go out in the evenings without me'; 'When we go to parties he ignores me'; 'I might just as well be a piece of furniture in the house'; 'She has no interest in my work'; 'She hardly seems to notice I'm around'. These people are all saying: 'I don't feel wanted'.

Well, the truth is that some of us need more proof of being wanted and loved than others. One wife, who values herself and is not over-dependent on what others think of her, can enjoy a party *in her own right* and allow her husband to enjoy it in his without feeling robbed of his regard.

Another, whose self-esteem is centred entirely in other people's view of her, feels sunk without trace if her husband, and to a lesser extent other people, are not appreciating her in overt ways *all the time*.

In between are the men and women who know most of the time that they are of value but are overwhelmed by a feeling of being cut-off, of being no importance to anyone, in certain situations.

It might be when something we have our own doubts about is called in question – like a piece of work we know we're not quite up to, or in situations which are universally daunting, like entering a roomful of strangers or beginning a public speech.

So it is important to realise that, in a sense, we are all ultimately alone. We cannot get rid of that 'unwanted feeling' by seeking more love, more attention, more admiration, more companionship from friends, marriage partner or children.

And if either of you does not basically think well of yourself, then the need to be thought well of is like a bottomless pit – all the loving attention and proof of love in the world is not enough to make you feel 'I am wanted' (see point 14).

This kind of shift from centring your opinion of yourself from others to inside yourself won't happen overnight. It means a slowly-gathering strength towards being more of a person in your own right.

But you can give it a good start by looking realistically at the occasions for that 'unwanted feeling'. 'Does he really go off in the evening to see his friends because he wants to get away from me? Or could it simply be that this is something he enjoys as *a person* which has nothing to do with how he feels about me, or I about him?'.

Similarly, a husband who feels 'unwanted' when his wife is devoting her attentions to the baby needs to ask himself: 'Does this really mean I'm of no importance to her? Or am I perhaps expecting and wanting for myself the kind of love she gives the baby? If my meal isn't ready, it might not be because she couldn't be bothered to get it for me. It might mean that she's just got behind with all these unfamiliar new jobs she has to do . . .'.

23 Deception or honesty?

The only practical way of dealing with these tricky questions: 'Should we tell each other everything?'; 'Is it better if we keep things to ourselves?' is to drop the 'all or nothing' approach.

In marriage, as in other relationships, it comes about naturally that we have some secret areas of our lives and others we need to share. This division occurs far more according to our own natures than to the demands of others.

But you will probably find that, as a marriage grows stronger, and the love and trust deepen, there may be more and more things you feel like moving from the secret areas into the shared one.

At first, however, there may be a dilemma about letting a loved-one know, for example, about previous loves and sexual experience (see point 40).

If you're a reserved sort of person and would rather not tell, there is really no law which says you must. Sometimes the need to 'confess' can be met just as well by telling someone else about it all – a clergyman, doctor or marriage guidance counsellor – than by telling your partner.

In this way, also, you are far more likely to get into perspective the feelings that made you want to confess, such as shame or guilt, which could be an unnecessary load to put onto your partner.

Later on, when it is *present* friendships, worries and feelings which you don't quite know whether to be honest about, it is really a matter of what kind of habit of communication you've built up.

By and large, the kind of honesty which is going to hurt the other person, and you know it will, ought to be recognised as not honesty at all but a form of hostility. 'You look awful in that dress' (when there's no time to change into another) is purely destructive. We all need, at times, the kindly sort of deception which enables us to have a good image of ourselves, even if it's only temporary.

It's not wrong, therefore, to deceive when the motive is loving – such as sparing worry or hurt. But it is a pity if the deception is happening when there is a need to share and when there is no certainty that the partner *will* be hurt or worried.

A husband or wife can be far more devastated to find that he or she was not trusted to share a worry, and help with it, than by the actual subject-matter of the worry. This even goes for extra-marital affairs. But deception or honesty about this is a much more complex problem (see point 26).

24 Jealousy

This is usually seen as a sign of love. 'Why, I do believe you're jealous!' is said with triumph and wonder as one might say: 'I do believe you really care for me . . .'.

Well, at this level it's no problem. Most of us, when we love someone, also have a slight sense of property about them. This makes us experience a twinge of fear when he or she gives undue attention to someone else, for there is always the possibility that he or she might prefer that someone else.

Most of us cannot help these little uncertainties and comparisons. It is a carry-over from the days when, as children, we occasionally felt that a brother or sister was preferred by our parents – and it felt very much as if we were about to lose their love.

The presence of this basic fear of losing love is why it's really very cruel for partners to whip up jealousy in each other. If you upset your wife by sighing over the pretty girls when you're out together, or anger your husband by praising another man's charm, the reaction is not a tribute. It merely confirms how afraid your partner is of losing love.

Although you may continue to sigh over pretty girls or swoon over other men's charms, if that's your nature, what your jealous partner needs is a lot more reassurance that this does nothing to alter the way you feel about him or her. In short, that he or she is loved.

There is also the deep-seated, suspicious form of jealousy. The wife or, more usually, the husband can hardly bear the partner to have any freedom at all.

Every trip to the shop is a visit to a lover, every letter is arranging an assignation – almost any sign that the other is a separate, self-governing person is seen as a threat to the security of this kind of person.

It is a sickeness and should be tackled as such. The only answer is for the sufferer himself, if he's aware of his problem, or his wife, if he isn't, to seek help from one of the helping agencies listed in Appendix A.

25 The hidden envy

This is the envy, in one degree or another, which each of us has for the opposite sex. Mostly, it remains hidden because it doesn't cause any trouble in people who are basically happy with their lives.

But it can crop up as a troublesome problem in marriage, as when a woman resents the biological facts or the assumptions that go with being a woman. It may take the form of rejecting a large part of a woman's life (refusal to have children or to make love or to bring up her children herself), or it can appear as a great fear of these functions.

If you have these fears, it's most important that you get the help you need. These feelings can't be willed out of existence, even if you want to be without them.

And if you just want to go on as you are, then for the sake of your husband, who is probably hoping very much for a normal married life and a family, it would be grown-up of you at least to go and talk over your fears with your own doctor, the woman doctor at the Family Planning Clinic or a marriage guidance counsellor.

In the home it's a commonplace fact that wives occasionally envy their husband's wider life outside, the travel and companionship and so on. And husbands often envy the woman's less demanding, passive role in the haven of home.

If there's a mutual understanding of these occasional longings, it needn't be any more of a problem than any other kind of wish or dream for 'things to be different'.

What it certainly *isn't* is an indication of homosexual feelings, which some partners are liable to read into it.

It's merely an expression of our bi-sexuality, the bit of feminine in every man, the bit of masculine in every woman. Where the longings are excessive, can't be accepted by either partner or are acted-on, then outside help is needed.

26 Infidelity

Infidelity can mean, to one wife, the fact that her husband takes a pretty, young secretary to lunch now and then, or drives her home. To another her husband is only 'unfaithful' if he actually has sexual intercourse with another woman. To a third, even this is not looked on as unacceptable infidelity unless he also falls in love with the other woman, and cuts his wife out of his affections to the point where she feels neglected and rejected.

There is no one answer, therefore, except this. If your partner is being unfaithful, you can only deal with it by finding out what it means to you, to him, to *your* marriage.

Never mind what it means to the world. Forget labels like 'adultery', 'eternal triangle', 'the other man' and 'the other woman'. These are situations, not people. You and your partner are people.

He was not unfaithful because 'husbands are like that' or because 'men want to have their cake and eat it'. She was not unfaithful because 'women are such romantic idiots'.

Each was unfaithful because, as a person, he or she looked for something which was not in the marriage, and which was needed sufficiently badly to risk breaking faith and causing all this upset and hurt.

So what was he looking for? The signs will have already been there in your relationship before the infidelity took place. For infidelity is a symptom of sickness in a marriage, not a sickness *per se*.

Was he feeling belittled, needing to feel ten feet tall instead? Was she hungry for tenderness? Was there a drifting apart or sexual coldness or indifference?

Infidelity is often a cry for help, which the other partner can either condemn or answer. Forgive and forget is not the answer. This just glosses over the 'whys' and 'wherefores'. Remember instead, and listen to each other. Not for too long though – only until it has enabled you both to see why it happened and reconstruct the 'missing parts' of your relationship.

Sometimes infidelity makes you too angry or hurt to ask 'why' at all, except perhaps: 'Why did he do this to me?'. And often other people's attitudes, or even your own, compel you to save face and feel revengeful or punishing instead of wanting to understand.

If this is the case, you may need help in starting the process of building up your marriage again. A marriage guidance counsellor would be the helper to approach.

27 The cold war

There are no rows or arguments. Love-making, if it takes place at all, is perfunctory and loveless. There is no praise or encouragement, but a lot of icy pointing-out of what isn't done or is done badly.

There is politeness; working arrangements for the family go smoothly and surface consideration is kept up. A good face is put on for the world, so that most of your friends, if asked, would say that yours was a 'happy marriage'.

Many marriages are like this. Everything has gone rather dead and cold, and underneath is a great deal of despair and unhappiness which the partners dare not admit to each other or to themselves.

If you want to leave it like this, no one can help you. There is no compulsion on any of us to live richly and fully if we would prefer to 'go through the motions' instead.

But if your unhappiness seeps through sometimes, as it must; if you sometimes feel you could love your partner and show it, if only you knew how; if you feel that perhaps your children have caught this 'coldness' and you fear for their ability, later on, to make happy relationships – then it really would be worth acknowledging that there is a problem and doing something about it.

It is never too late.

You could start off by reading something about love and marriage and relationships. Appendix B will help you with this. Or you might want to talk things over with someone selected and trained to counsel people with emotional problems. This is what Marriage Guidance Councils are for.

part iii The Outside World

This part is about problems which can crop up in a husband's and wife's dealings with the outside world, but which have to be settled by them *together* if they are not to turn into problems for their 'inside' world too.

28 Where to live

You'll find, if you think hard about it, that you have in your mind's eye an image of the ideal home. You may long to recreate a happy home of the past – your own childhood home or the one you dreamed of then, a place you visited on holiday or something you read about in a book.

You may have a longing for a rustic, isolated spot or to be among other people in a busy town, to be near your old home or to get as far away from it as possible. Your partner will have his 'ideal' too, and it may be very different from yours, although on the surface you may delight in the fact that 'we like the same things'.

Mostly, being sober voting citizens and proud of coping with life in a realistic way, we keep these dreams well suppressed. But now and again, when the effort at compromising seems too much, they burst out and a conflict arises between your dream and the other's dream – although it's seldom dealt with in these terms and it might be better if it were.

The forms it takes are: 'She won't leave the town and I want to live in the country', or 'She wants to start off in her mother's place and I'm all for scratching along in one room' or 'He wants to go to Australia and she can't bear to leave England', or 'He's dying to retire to Devon and I want to stay here'.

The only thing to do, when this happens, is to accept together that no move is irrevocable. The world has shrunk, we're all much more mobile and we don't actually put down roots. One dream attempted and found wanting is better than a compromise which makes no one's dream possible.

If, for instance, he hankers after the country and she wants a Kensington flat – assuming that either is possible from the point of view of money and work – and they both 'give and take' only so far as to settle for literally half-way between, i.e. in the suburbs, then you've got two losers and a very explosive situation.

But to be able to decide in either of the other directions – for his country cottage or her town flat, they need not only to explore the realities of the situation but also to explore and chew over the feelings involved.

Her only objections to the country may be found, in discussion, to be fear of loneliness and being 'cut off', of becoming a cabbage. So it's worth cultivating friends who live as you hope to live – in a cottage, in a town flat – before you accept that these fears can't be overcome or are anything more than fears of the unknown.

There's one danger point that arises in the early days of marriage – but which can also recur throughout the marriage if it's given its head earlier on. When love is blooming and there's a tremendous wish to give the other the moon, this makes one partner so flexible that he or she will stifle their own feelings about 'nest-building', or defining the territory they hope to occupy, and simply say 'We'll go wherever you want' – and resent it fiercely afterwards.

The end of that particular road is the air of martyrdom and a great deal of niggling dissatisfaction, which find their outlet in other directions – in bed, for instance.

So any problem about where to live is already moving towards a solution if you're not afraid to air your wishes and your dreams too. Then, and only then, can you find you're willing to postpone them, fit them into reality or give them a try. If they stay unexpressed, they stay as dreams which you'll begin to feel your partner has wilfully killed or stolen from you.

29 Setting-up home

Most problems about setting-up home usually arise out of the expectations which either partner brings to the marriage which don't stand up to the demands of reality (see point 1).

Even if money's not tight – the most limiting factor on anyone's expectations – there are all kinds of ideas about how a home should look, what it should have in it and how it's run, which have more to do with the blandishments of advertising than with real life.

Sometimes it's difficult to recognise this, for what the image of the ideal home does so well, and so disastrously for our peace of mind, is to feed that compulsion which is in all of us, to some degree, towards making order out of chaos, controlling our environment and magically wishing perfection into our daily lives.

Understand this and you'll understand the apparently ludicrous despair of the wife who finds the new lampshade doesn't match the curtains, or the husband who chokes with rage at the lop-sided way the electrician fitted the light-switch. Few of us are much good at tolerating failure and frustration in the one area over which we feel we ought to have absolute control – the home.

But this is something that we all have to do in the end or end up as obsessionally houseproud women, driving the family to misery with the constant emptying of ash-trays, shrieks to wipe your feet, and refusals of help 'because you don't do it right', or as tartars of husbands who can't bear to read the evening paper if someone else has 'got at it' first and put a crease in page four.

If there's any problem then, which has nothing to do with money, about setting up home, the answer will usually lie in a willingness to 'let go' of the drive towards perfection and tolerate the occasional muddle and mess that real life so often is.

You'll need to compromise more than you thought, settle for the next best, take in your stride gadgets which don't work, furniture which turned out to be a bad buy, even the picture he or she drools over which makes you feel sick.

But the best way round it is to find all these things funny rather than tragic – and that isn't at all difficult unless you're bent on seeing that life gives you a raw deal. But that's a different, bigger problem (see point 79).

30 Moving home

Most peoples' feelings about big changes in their lives, especially those which involve an entire change in environment, such as emigrating, are apt to bring into play the feelings they had in original situations of the same kind from way back. The first day at school; the prospect of leaving home; the last few weeks before the marriage. Some of us see these moves as challenges and go to meet them with confidence. Others of us always have had some difficulty in facing new situations and have to overcome a feeling of insecurity before we can settle into a new life.

So, if there is any conflict about moving home, it is important to look beyond the apparent pig-headedness, or the 'childish' reluctance to swap the known for the unknown.

Most often it is the wife who lets go less easily of what is familiar; but it can happen to men too, as in the case of men who refuse promotion or a job overseas although the wife may be willing to make the changes this involves.

Once you have really bothered to find out what perfectly natural fears and feelings lie behind a conflict like this, and accept them, it's surprising how very much easier it is for the other person to overcome them. What we are forced to deny, we can never fight. What we can admit to and have understood is capable of being beaten.

31 Whose name on the cheques?

Let's face it – any real problem about money can only be actually solved by having more of it . . . or working things out so well that you don't feel so short of it (see 101 Ways to Manage your Money. Details in Appendix B).

What we're concerned about here is a solution to the problem of arguments about money – who pays for what, resentment at an unalterable financial position, that hopeless position in which it's control of the money that's at issue, and the needs of each partner, both for spending and for saving, as a means to a sense of security.

Two things need to be said. No matter whether only one or both of the partners are contributing money to the marriage, they both need to have the responsibility, and the means to use this responsibility, for running the home.

This does mean either a joint account (even if there are also separate accounts) or access to a fixed sum without constant referral to each other on every item. There has to be this basic trust.

Sometimes, of course, it's misplaced. A husband will empty the household account for fun-buys of his own. Or a wife will turn hopelessly extravagant (see point 78). This is nearly always for emotional reasons and needs measures of its own (see points 77 and 78). But basically, the answer to the problem of whose name on the cheque is – both. If one or other partner is utterly against this mutual trust and freedom, then they need to look for the answer to their problem in the area of power rather than of money (see point 17).

32 Budgeting

Problems about budgeting are not only about where to lay out enough money to best effect but also about the feelings of the husband and wife concerning what they value most and how they have been used to spending money in the past.

A husband who has never had to fend for himself has had no opportunity to learn the basic facts about housekeeping. To him, food on the table, scouring powder in the bathroom and a plentiful supply of towels is not seen as pounds, shillings and pence. He has no idea of what it takes to run a home – and it's the easiest thing in the world for him to feel that it should cost less.

The only solution here, if there are disagreements about where the money goes, is for the wife occasionally to write a list of everything spent in one week, right from the milk bill to the stamp for a child's thank-you letter.

Sometimes, too, we have magic feelings about money – that it is elastic, or will somehow turn up to meet the bill for things we want so desperately that they almost become a right. It is always fatal, then, not at some time or another to put it down firmly in black and white. Then both partners can see that they are indeed spending £x a week on dog-food and moaning about not having enough for a washing machine on hire-purchase.

The choice may never have been made; it just happened. And it can be valuable to get things so straight that choices can be made in a definite clear-eyed way. They must not be allowed to make themselves with all the resentment this brings.

It's a nasty feeling when you realise that spending is controlling you instead of you controlling the spending and it tends to make you blame the other half of the non-controlling team.

A lot of action can be taken to get budgeting on a better footing with limited room for self-indulgent spending on either side. (I'd recommend some room being left for self-indulgent spending – we all need a bit of that).

There are, for example, budgeting accounts run by most banks where enough is put into the account monthly to meet all the household bills over the year.

Another problem is when too much stress has been put on the 'togetherness' thing. It often happens that one partner enjoys working out the money and being responsible for the bills, and is good at it, whereas the other does not and isn't.

There's no reason why this area shouldn't be taken over entirely by the partner who likes it – provided the other is happy about this, and provided the one who's doing it doesn't later accuse the other of laziness, but remembers that he or she chose to do it.

33 The housekeeping money

There's only one problem about housekeeping money — and that's that it isn't enough.

But enough for what? That's the point. On examination it will be found that mostly this is not a question of going without necessities but of the amount not being enough to cover the wife's standards or ideas about how her home should be. These can be far in excess of what the husband wants, or, indeed, of what he can afford.

Any conflict about housekeeping money can only begin to be solved, therefore, by an honest appraisal of what each expects from everyday life. If the wife has unrealistic ideas of what can be managed on what she's given — such as thinking that steak can be staple fare for a family on an income of £15 — then she badly needs some useful instruction on how to feed and care for a family within the limits. There are suggestions for help with this among the recommended literature at the end of this book.

But reality is different for everyone. A wife who's accustomed from childhood to seeing curtains replaced when they get worn (or merely boring) will take this spending as such a matter of course that she will seldom question whether money will stretch to it.

She may need to find, in discussion with her husband, that for him new curtains are considered a rare treat and looked on as totally unnecessary beside the importance, for example, of keeping the family car in running order. And, the way their life is in reality, his priorities may be more practical than hers are. So housekeeping is very much a matter of seeing what is, and not 'what might be' or 'what ought to be' (see point 32).

Where housekeeping money is simply not forthcoming, or being gambled away (see point 94) or is witheld as part of a deeper war between the partners, then some form of outside help has to be sought, especially where there are children.

The Probation Officer helps with problems of this kind, so do marriage guidance counsellors and, where there is resulting hardship for wife or children, the local welfare authorities.

34 The car

Having a car solves a lot of problems but it seems to bring a good many too. 'He spends all his spare time tinkering with the car' is the problem of a lot of wives. Or even: 'He loves his car more than me'.

There is also the growing number of wives who are worried by a husband's aggressive or dangerous way of driving when he's under stress.

Many families are so dependent on a car that it must be maintained and repaired, often at an expense greater than they can reasonably afford, and this leads to a niggling feeling that the blessing is also a millstone.

We cannot turn back the clock. So it's pointless now to regret that the car has become such an important symbol for the owner that it is almost an extension of his personality. It represents his image of himself and he will invest in it all the emotions that don't find more satisfying targets elsewhere.

Women do not, on the whole, see a car as a symbol of anything – not their own car anyway. It's simply a vehicle which gets them from place to place and all that's required is that it should work reliably.

But for modern man, deprived of the hunt and the chase, and of primitive ways of expressing rivalry and aggression, the car which can overtake another car, look longer, look bigger, get there first, is a sign of his own manliness and triumph over other men. Wives just have to recognize this. Civilization has so often left a man no alternative.

But obviously it's better, realising this, to avoid situations in which the car can be seen as a weapon or taken as an outlet for anger in a way that is dangerous to others.

It takes self-control, but I believe a man should not be allowed to go out and drive after a row at home (no more than after too much drink) or, to put it the right way round, rows should be avoided before driving.

And an argument in the car should be absolutely avoided. It shouldn't be beyond the common-sense of most partners to co-operate on this for their own peace of mind – and safety!

35 Status and possessions

It's hard for us not to see different standards of living, in the material sense, as better standards. This is because most of us are so uncertain about where we stand and what people think of us, and over-concerned about both these issues.

So if there is a noticeable difference between our status and somebody else's – they have a swimming-pool and we don't – it's fatally easy to see this as 'better' and therefore something to be striven for until we too are 'better' – both better than we were and better than other people who don't have a swimming-pool.

How often this kind of move depends more on status-seeking than on the realities of their own life and needs, only a husband and wife themselves know – but it is important that they *do* know.

There is an enormous pressure on us now to gather up more material goods and it takes a pretty strong character to pause and think and decide 'But we don't actually need that and shan't be any the worse without it.'

We all have fantasies about a possible life in which the wants and discomforts of this one are removed. Some of these fantasies are pure pipe-dreams and recognised as unattainable – like the longing of the wife in a semi-detached to live in a villa in St. Tropez.

But others are believed to be attainable – it is part of human nature to strive for them – and it really is vital that each partner knows and can tell the other what his or her particular expectations of life are.

All the problems about 'Why on earth did you go and buy such an enormous fridge?' and 'Do you really want to spend all that money on a picture?' just couldn't arise if we were given access to each other's private dreams.

Maybe the picture-buyer sees himself as a patron of the arts or he's someone who 'could have painted'. Maybe she only feels safe if she has a week's supply of food in the fridge at any moment – these are feelings which are part of the marriage and govern the partners' attitudes to possessions and to their role among friends and neighbours as well as to each other.

When it doesn't really matter, we should allow each other some expression of our dreams. When it does matter – such as when you can't afford even the tiniest expression of a dream – you can still recognise and allow the dream itself.

'Wouldn't it be lovely if . . .' is not a threat to anyone. A marriage partner is really doing a lot for the other if he can agree 'Yes, it would', rather than damning her for having expensive dreams.

36 The claims of his job

When a wife complains that her husband 'puts his job before me', there really is no answer except to say 'And so he should.' Her problem is not that he does that, for all men must put their living before their loving, but that she feels so rejected and miserable about it. The problem and its answer is entirely within her.

Clearly no-one is going to feel miserable about the way someone else spends his time if she has satisfactory ways of passing the time herself. And this is the only way. One cannot make a husband hurry home from work unless he's pretty interested in what he's going to find when he gets there.

It might be the food, the comfort and attractiveness of the house, the friends who are coming in to dinner – or it might be the wife herself. But she's got to be pretty interesting to keep him that interested in her alone and this certainly won't come from moping about how lonely she is.

She'd have to start being a person in her own right, even if she's tied to the home by young children. A mind is not tied. It's the freest thing we have. It can roam all over the place while its owner is at the sink or by the fire. And when it's no longer dependent on a husband's company for all its stimulation and delight, that's very likely when she'll get a great deal more of that company.

Some jobs take a man from home for long periods and there's no doubt that this can raise some problems in a marriage if the wife is very unsure of herself and of him and imagines he's being unfaithful. But it's still no answer for him to stay at home, even if his job allowed it.

The answer is for her to cultivate the ability to be a separate person, not wholly dependent on another person nor being more complete when he's there, but being complete and interested in life most of the time and just *happier* when he's there – which is a different matter from feeling lost and unhappy when he isn't.

The claims of a man's job, therefore, are not a problem – they are life and they have to be adapted to even when, or especially when, the claims are a cover for a reluctance to be at home.

37 The claims of her job

The claims of a woman's job can give rise to problems too, but they are not the same problems and can't be answered in the same way.

Unfortunately the roles of a man and woman in married and family life are not the same and never can be. Women may wish like mad that a husband's attitude to her work and to her being out of the house for most of the day (perhaps even when he comes home) is the same as her attitude to his going out to work – but it is not.

We are biological creatures and a man expects in his very

bones for woman to be the comfort, the warmth, the food-giver, the background to his life that the first woman was – his mother.

It is, after all, equally in a woman's bones to expect the man in her life to provide the basic essentials with which her father endowed the family – the means to live, the roof over their heads, the protection and responsibility and pillar of strength.

So much are these things in our bones that it doesn't matter whether our real parents were like this or not – if they were, they will continue to serve as models for the ideal. If they weren't, we will seek in a partner all the more eagerly those qualities which we missed in childhood.

These things are not conscious. When a man comes home from work, rather like the boy from school, and there is no-one in the house, the fire is out and he must make his own cup of tea, he does not consciously think: 'I wish I had a wife who wasn't working'. He only knows that something is missing.

Perhaps this has to be; women cannot always fulfil themselves *and* arrange to be with the kettle boiling just when needed. But it is vitally important to realise that these feelings are there.

They explain a lot of the resentment a man feels about his wife's success in a job, the fierce competitiveness that can flare up, and the inferiority he feels when she earns more than he does and makes no bones about it.

To him this is no longer a partner, matching her role to his; it is a rival for his role and it takes enormous confidence to sort this out and come to terms with it.

Couples are doing this now; but it will take time. Meanwhile, it's a big help if a wife doesn't crow about the claims of her job, and if her husband can accept that if she has a job, it does have claims on her to which he'll have to give way.

part iv Other People

Other people are often said to be 'the only problem a marriage has'. 'Our marriage would be perfectly happy if it weren't for his mother, her sister, my father, our neighbour, the boss, the landlady etc etc.'

But it's not that being married raises difficulties about different relationships. Life does. What these people are saying is: 'Life would be perfect if it weren't for his mother, her sister, etc ...'

Life requires us to enter into relationships other than with one person of the opposite sex and our joint off-spring. And marriage, far from restricting the sorrows and joys of relationships with others into a mere bond of two — as is fondly hoped in the honeymoon stage ('just you and me at last') — actually widens our contact with a variety of other people in an ever more complex set of relationships.

Each of us can only manage these as successfully or as unhappily as we are accustomed to manage relationships in general — other than falling in love. Falling in love is easy. It's no guide to a person's ability to love, tolerate and relate to other people. And the demands of the other person are no guide either. Some wives get on like a house on fire with a truly possessive mother-in-law; others seem to make a hash of relating to a real dear.

So when there is a problem about another person the really valuable first move is to ponder: 'Well, first, is there something I'm doing or expecting or not seeing quite straight which is causing a bit of the trouble?'. Let's see how this works with some of the 'other people' on the fringe of a marriage.

38 Mother-in-law

The old jokes don't raise quite the laugh they used to, so perhaps this is not such an uneasy relationship as it used to be. But it isn't always too easy.

The problem is usually seen as interference by the mother-in-law or her dependence on the company of the married son or daughter.

"She's always round here', or 'My wife's always expected up there', or 'He visits his mother twice a week and does all her odd jobs' or 'She tells me how to manage the kids, what to cook, etc'.

But, of course, any relationship is a two-way thing, even if your part in it is resentment and hate. So one way of tackling this difficulty is to look at the part played by the married partner whose mother is always visiting or always being visited.

Even if a husband appears to resent his own mother's constant presence, or a wife goes reluctantly to visit her mother two or three times a week, neither of them has *actually* found a way of cutting loose from this close tie with the parent.

They have their own problems of simply *not being able* to limit the large slice of their lives which mother is still controlling. It is a problem we all go through, at some stage in our lives, this loosening of the bonds with parents. We think we are mainly struggling to break *their* hold over us but we are also struggling to loosen *our* own hold on them.

When this isn't managed, then the bond that remains is likely to be charged as much with hate and resentment as with love and dependence. No wonder husbands and wives often don't quite know what their feelings are about a mother who's always around and therefore take it out on each other.

It takes a grown-up person to handle this situation so that no one is hurt and the ties are loosened on both sides. But marriage is for grown-ups. And the bonds have to be loosened by love and not by force.

What do you do? Well, it is first up to the son or daughter to accept that the intrusion by mother-in-law into the marriage *is* distressing to the other partner. Sometimes this is bad enough for the partner to feel that the other does not really *belong* to the marriage but still has one foot in his or her old life and home.

It is not difficult to understand how painful this feeling is for anyone who loves you and puts you first and wants very much to feel that you love him or her and put him/her first.

Move over to her side a little more and start to see it with her eyes. Then you can begin to tackle the actual difficulties.

Perhaps the mother-in-law in question is lonely. She still, perhaps, feels unwanted and useless if she's not having a good say in her child's life. So one answer may be to steer her towards friends and interests on her own account. You may find you need to go through a period of *inviting* her over several times to switch the relationship from one on her terms to one on yours.

By the same token you could start asking for advice and help now and again, offering to do odd jobs, on the principle that if you can *give* her the feeling of still being needed in a small area, she will not have to *take* for herself such a large one.

In other words it is often up to a married couple, however late in the day, to help an in-law into her role and see that she enjoys it.

This is all the more necessary when, as so often happens, her own marriage has somehow failed her or she's a widow or has always put more interest and affection on to her children than on to her husband.

The difficulty then, and it is a very real one for all that it is unconscious, is in letting her children go. And it is often not until they are married that she is faced with this task and is unable to cope with it.

What we hope one day to do for our children – to set them free as individuals to lead their own lives – we may often have first to help our in-laws to do for us and our partners.

It's not too much to ask of grown-up people who understand what is happening. And this is all it needs – to be adult and to understand.

If you have a father-in-law problem – which is rather rare – perhaps the next point will help you.

39 Other relations

There can be problems here – and invariably are. A sister of the husband whom the wife can't take to (or the sister can't take to the wife), a brother of either who uses the place as a second home, maybe a boozy uncle, a dominating grandmother or a cousin who just grates.

As men are able to be more casual about relationships and, to be utterly practical, have to do very much less of the work entailed in keeping them up – the arrangements, the cooking, feeding, fetching and carrying etc. – it is not too difficult for them either to opt out of relationships that are not too welcome, or to tolerate them at an aloof level.

They can find a job in the garden when the awkward sister calls or merely sit behind the paper when a chatty aunt drones on.

But, for the wife, two opposing feelings are usually at work. Most women have a keen desire to keep family relationships a going concern as a general principle. They like to feel that members of the larger family are in touch with each other and loosely held together.

It gives them a feeling of continuity and security, so that even members of their own family with whom, at heart, they are not too harmonious, are kept in warm storage in between occasional rituals like Christmas, weddings and so on.

The opposing feeling is the here-and-now resentment, when the irritating relative is actually in the house and must be attended to, listened to, lived with for an hour or two. This demands tolerance.

She might find she can be more tolerant of the relation as an individual instead of seeing him or her just as a splinter off a central mass called 'My family' or 'His family'.

But one thing we don't always take into account when this problem comes up, is the simple old cliché that 'it takes all sorts to make a world'. We all feel more comfortable on the whole with 'people like us'. Marriage brings into your circle people who may not be what, up to now, has been 'your sort of person'.

If they are relations of your husband or wife, they are already in the world of your partner and have not been *chosen* by you as friends or acquaintances. This makes it a little more difficult to rub along with them.

But if you're a happy person, you can rub along with anyone in small doses. So keep the doses small if you don't honestly welcome any particular person.

If you're an unhappy person, then that will certainly be reflected in your ability to rub along with people you haven't chosen as friends.

If relations, therefore, begin to jangle your nerves and strain your tolerance unbearably, the cause is likely to be in *you* rather than in *them*. If you can put your finger on what's really getting at you (sex relations gone awry? a battle of wills over money going on?), then you'll find help for that under another heading in this book.

40 Past loves

The constructive way to look at any past loves of a man or woman is that, good or bad, right or wrong, they are part of that person. They helped to make them what they are; maybe they produced fears and hurt; or they added to their strength and well-being and self-esteem. Whatever it was, those who experienced them took these relationships into themselves in their own way and they are now part of them.

Well, that's fine. Someone who loves that person will, quite naturally, like to know about previous relationships. It is like asking: 'What have you felt? What are you made of?' It is fascinating, in fact, to find out why someone you love is as she is or he is. It is part of loving, to perceive someone in this way as the sum of their experiences.

But, alas, it takes a confident person to love and accept in this way. Someone with little confidence, little certainty about his own ability to love and be loved, cannot help seeing anything which has been given to or added to the beloved as something which has been taken away from *him*.

This applies even if it happened years before they met. It's not logical. It's not rational. Like a lot of feelings, it's just crazy. But it's no use thinking you can overcome this particular form of jealousy by rational, logical means.

'Yes, darling, I did love him/her but I didn't know you then' or 'I wouldn't have done if I'd met you first', or 'Why must you keep harping on that!' gets you nowhere.

The jealous partner, afraid and ashamed of his own possessiveness, is really only wanting to hear, over and over: 'Yes, I loved him but I love you more than him'; 'That woman was loved, yes, but now you are loved more'. This needs to be shown so often in so many consistent, everyday ways that the partner who is on such shaky ground can at least feel that nothing has been taken from him or is going to be. We operate our own loss-making machines (see point 24).

A lot to ask of a partner, to treat you with such compassion and understanding, when maybe she would like this herself!

The only answer to this is that if you give these things, you get them – you married a human being and every one of us has some area in which we feel on shaky ground and need reassurance.

41 Living with in-laws

In a word, the answer to this is – don't. Sometimes we try to kid ourselves that, just like the Chinese or the Italians or all the other splendid examples of respect and affection between several generations of one family, we really can manage to share living-space with other branches of the family. But we are not like this. It is not in our bones; although it may sometimes work out well later in mellow middle-age.

In this country the pattern is for newly-weds to break away from the parent's world, emotionally and physically, and start up a new family. In other countries this does not always happen – a wife can still be 'the daughter of the house' as well and combine the two rôles without friction. Or the husband remains 'the first son' as well as husband and everything goes smoothly.

But here we make great claims on a marriage partner to put his or her 'old home', parental ties and emotional dependencies behind him.

So there is inevitable friction in the context of starting married life in his home or her home. And I really think the only way to avoid it, if there is no alternative, is to set a limit to the stay and stick to it. It must be for six months or one year, not 'until we get our own place' or 'until the first child'.

There are couples who, without actively planning to do so, have put off their own place or their first child simply because the *status quo* became the easier course.

Another tip is to start off on a very business-like footing. No matter how darling mother is, how beautifully husband fits in, sit down and work out the lines of demarcation – who pays for what, who cooks what, where privacy can be guaranteed, who's first for the bathroom and just what each member of the family means by sharing.

No use father secretly hoping son-in-law will cut the lawn in exchange for not having to pay for the landing light – he'll just have to say this is what he's hoping for and see if he's agreeable.

The only real problems of co-existence are failures in communicating your wants and expectations. So get everything clear and business-like – this applies especially where everyone likes each other and it's all warm and close and 'we'll all get on beautifully'. Better to mark out the territory and responsibilities first and there'll be considerably less chance of problems.

42 Friends who advise

Friends amount to a problem, it seems, when, out of genuine sympathy or a wish to help, they begin to take a part in your marriage problems and crises.

Unfortunately it is almost impossible for a friend to stay a friend once he or she has taken sides in a marriage dispute, even if it was *your* side.

On the unimportant level, it's fine to have friends to whom one can moan 'Do you know what he did the other day?' and to have the friend say: 'Isn't it awful! Mine behaves just the same at times'.

What one doesn't want, and shouldn't ever offer, is the active and biassed response such as: 'Did he do that! Well, it must be awful for you. I've always thought he was rather mean. I don't know how you cope'. It may warm the cockles of your heart for the moment, and make your grievance feel comfortable to you, but later on the grievance will be turned against the friend. That's the way it goes.

With serious marriage problems it can be far worse. A friend who wants to do more than listen and help you off-load your hurt may move right over into your problem with: 'I should do this if I were you'.

She's playing with fire. What other people feel about how you've behaved or how your partner has behaved has nothing to do with your problem. It is how you feel that's important.

This is why friends fulfil their function if they give you their warmth and support as a background without entering into your problem.

For the kind of detached guidance which enables you to make your own decisions on the basis of your own way of looking at things it's best to go to a probation officer or marriage guidance counsellor or some other impartial helper. He won't make the mistake of thinking that his own attitudes and experiences have the slightest bearing on your individual problem.

There is also a strong streak in all of us tending towards 'saving face' in front of friends. In marriage disputes, therefore, we're not, when discussing them with friends, so much concerned with solving a problem as with justifying our side of the matter, putting ourselves in the right and preserving our self-esteem and pride.

Friends, without meaning to, are inclined to inflame these feelings with remarks like: 'I shouldn't let him get away with that. . .'. Many a separation or divorce has come about simply through this compulsion on the part of one partner to 'do the right thing' in the eyes of friends and avoid appearing weak or humiliated.

So the answer is to avoid friends who give advice, or, if they are otherwise good friends, ignore the advice. And don't give any yourself. Just listen. That's, after all, what friends are for.

43 The friends you can't take to

Different people have different tastes in friends. Even twins have different tastes in friends and lovers, once they're allowed to be individuals. So it's inevitable that a husband may enjoy the company of a man his wife hasn't much time for and that his wife should have a woman friend or two who leave the husband cold.

The only times this really becomes a problem is when one of the partners, or both, have the unconscious feeling that, because they are united in marriage, they are united, as one person, in other things.

They expect the partner to have the same feelings about people as he or she has. 'I like old Joe, so why can't she?'; 'Joan's such a nice person, why can't he see it?'

It *is* difficult for some partners to acknowledge the separateness of people, and to tolerate their differences in attitude and feeling, to allow the other the freedom to like and dislike completely different things and people. For some, this difference seems like a threat: 'He likes Joe better than he likes me'; 'That woman's always round here when I come home. It's more her home than mine'.

If the feeling of being threatened or the jealousy is there, it can't easily be shaken off without a change in attitude somewhat along these lines: 'He's himself and I'm myself, and we aren't the same people so, of course, he sees Joe in his way and I see him in mine. He's taking nothing from me by liking Joe. But I certainly take something from him if I won't allow him to like Joe'.

Then it really can become easy to say candidly: 'Well, he's not my cup of tea but I can quite understand that he's yours'. And the more freedom your partner has to like different people, the less he'll want to try to make you like them too.

There'll be less foisting of each other's friends on the other and certainly less of those tiresome guilt-feelings which make him sneak off to see Joe on some other excuse or make her shove Joan out of the kitchen just as his car's heard outside.

This is a pretty rotten way to live anyway. The alternative, with tolerance for your partner's difference and separateness, brings enormous rewards to the whole marriage in a more loving and open response to life.

44 Flirtations

Obviously this isn't a problem for the partner who's doing the flirting. It's therefore no answer to strive to stop him or her from flirting, as one might hope, for example, to cure a man of drinking too much or a woman of buying three dresses every time she sets out to buy one.

On the contrary, the pleasures of flirting are so great both for the initiator and the object of his flirting and, to my mind, so harmless, that it's difficult not to see it as a positive asset rather than a drawback.

Socially, there's no doubt that the man who makes a woman feel admired and wanted, even for half an hour, and the woman who makes a man feel the same, are adding something to the sum of human happiness.

But there is a problem when the partner doesn't see it that way. And the question then is not how to stop the flirting but how to come to terms with it. The only way to do this is to work out on what factors the objections are based.

Most likely on fear – fear that in paying attention to other members of the opposite sex the partner is saying he prefers them to his own wife or her own husband.

But most flirtatious people have an obvious liking for the entire opposite sex – they enjoy the moves and counter-moves in 'the sex game'. They are, mainly, generous and confident in their feelings towards people and are likely to show this in their married life.

For my money, this is preferable to the partner who has difficulty in loving and admiring and giving his feelings. The partner of a flirt is actually in a pretty enviable position – the chosen mate of a man or woman who enjoys the opposite sex in an outgoing, straightforward way.

There is also the fear that mild flirtations may lead to serious affairs – a partner may particularly fear this if he or she has been let down in the past.

But the flirt simply likes to flirt. He makes his own escapes from situations which look like being taken too seriously. The man or woman who basically wants to get involved is a horse of a different colour entirely and he is not interested in spreading his warm heart around a party (see point 26 and also 99).

45 Trouble with the neighbours

Annoyances from neighbours can happen. Housewives have their different limits of tolerance for the noise other people's children make, blaring television sets, washing-lines perpetually obscuring the view, dogs tied up and barking all day while the owners are at work, or the neighbour who seems to demand too much in the way of taking in her laundry or supplying provisions she's run out of.

But this is rarely a marriage problem unless the husband, who does not himself have to suffer the annoyances, is completely unsympathetic to the difficulties. He may simply not want to be bothered and will therefore take the line that it's 'all a mountain out of a mole-hill'.

Or he may suspect that his wife is working up a great deal of indignation which can lead to unpleasantness and would rather she put up with it than tried to do something about it. In either case her annoyance and sense of persecution is likely to be magnified and turned on to him through sheer blocking of any way out.

But what astonishes most people who've had a problem of this kind is how easily it's been overcome by a joint friendly approach from husband and wife. What has seemed like callous indifference to their peace or comfort invariably turns out to be a case of the neighbours simply not knowing that anyone else was affected by the nuisance, far less doing it deliberately to annoy.

It is extraordinarily easy to breed either ill-will or good-will in neighbours simply by what one expects of them. And it's here that a husband can answer this problem.

Free of the sense of persecution his wife may have from the daily annoyance, he can introduce the idea of there being good-will both in the approach and in the likely neighbourly response.

And if this fails – or the neighbour's children have nowhere else to play, or their grandfather is deaf and must have the television on loud – then a husband can still do his bit by recognising that this is something his wife has to learn to live with and tolerate rather than refusing to believe any annoyance exists.

'I think it's marvellous the way you cope with it' is a lot more helpful than: 'It can't be as bad as all that' – and it costs no more.

46 His boss

One hears alarming rumours from America that some large firms reckon that when they take a man into employment, they're virtually taking on his wife too – the reasoning being that how he works and his attitude to promotion and authority might be quite a bit dependent on what sort of person his wife is.

In cases like this, where the wife is interviewed too, you could say that a man's marriage is brought right into his working area and that his boss's judgement of his wife – and vice versa – is every bit as important as his boss's judgement of him.

Personally, I find this rather nauseating. I think it fairly important that the traffic between a man's work and his personal relationships should be strictly one way. His feelings about his work and his boss are, if he chooses, brought into the marriage situation and not the other way round – except at the superficial social level where the two areas may occasionally join up, say, at an office party or when the boss and his wife come to dinner.

It is important that at home he should be able to moan about the odd injustice, misunderstanding, grievance and outright hostility to his boss. These feelings are inevitable in the relationship between employer and employee.

Wives sometimes get worried by this letting-off steam, believing it to represent a wholesale discontent with the job and hatred of the boss. But all it means is that she's getting the side of the picture that he cannot express at work or to his colleagues.

This applies even if his boss is a veritable saint – a man can rarely be under another's direct authority without needing to reduce his boss's power just a little, either in fantasy or out loud at his own hearth. There will be few problems about 'his boss' if a wife can recognise this and simply listen with understanding.

47 Her boss

Her boss can be more of a problem. It's a comparatively new situation for men to face – this presence of another man in the wife's daily life who has some authority over her and to whom she has obligations and duties.

There seem to be less problems when the wife's boss is a woman – which makes it look as if there is an element of sexual jealousy in it, much as there is when a wife has mixed feelings about her husband's secretary.

When there are basic objections to the wife working at all, then obviously a lot of the resentment will be directed at the wife's boss. If she's working as a secretary, her boss is clearly getting 'cared for' and attended to, and a husband who feels neglected is bound to see the boss as taking his place, even though the attentions he receives are of a completely different nature.

When there are no objections to the wife working, the money's welcome and a good modus vivendi has been worked out at home, a husband can still have unconscious objections to the wife's boss for primitive, biological reasons.

The tradition of a woman being dependent on man and living through man is so strong that it is hard for a man to understand a woman having an independent, asexual and business-like relationship with other men.

The fact is that many women cannot manage this yet — there are still many who do fall in love with their bosses or are, deep down, wanting admiration and attention from the men they work with. This, of course, makes it more difficult for a husband to accept that his wife, or any wife, can work for a man without switching emotional interests from the marriage and family.

The answer? It depends mostly on the husband. If he's a confident man, secure in his own job and in his wife's love, you can talk about your work and your boss with freedom, as a husband does.

If, on the other hand, he has problems about competitiveness, jealousy or fears of being neglected and 'left out', then it's sensible to keep your work-worries in the background, including any brickbats or bouquets for your boss.

48 Working colleagues

Husband and wives often have the same problems about the others' working colleagues which they have about friends, i.e. that they may tolerate them in small doses but often don't care for them to be always about.

Unfortunately, some men with no outside interests may have no friends except the people they work with. Whereas women, even if they have no job outside the home, are more likely to have a mixed bag of friends, made up of neighbours, parents of children the same age as their own, a woman or two from the old working days and even a girl they were at school with.

If it gets to the stage where all the people you have drinks with or entertain are people your husband works with and there's nothing talked but 'shop', it would seem a good idea to find out whether he's quite happy about this or whether he might, in fact, welcome a bit of a shake-up on your initiative.

Enclosed circles of friends, in which all the points of view are known and a continuous familiar dialogue is actually taking place at every meeting, may be a safe and cosy way of socializing but it can lead to a rut which is a bit sad when the people who are in the rut are not aware of it or don't want to budge.

It often happens that the spontaneous new friendship — on holiday, through the childrens' school or in any way outside the job – proves to be the most rewarding and leads a husband and wife to regret missing other opportunities of widening their horizons and relationships.

49 The best friend

There seems to be something singularly attractive about the best friend: 'I've fallen in love with my husband's best friend'; 'I've discovered that my husband is having an affair with my best friend'; and, before marriage: 'My best friend has been going out with my fiancé' or, starkly: 'My best friend has stolen my boy'.

Well, it happens. Obviously, the reason that it happens is partly one of opportunity. If a man or woman is dissatisfied with his or her present relationship and unconsciously on the search for one that would seem to be more satisfying, then the 'best friend', who is around and is already friendly and perhaps appreciative, becomes an obvious target.

This is especially true for the man or woman who's uncertain about forming completely new relationships from square one — or is basically lazy.

So the question is not: 'How could he betray me with my best friend?' but 'Why is he betraying me at all?'. Given the fact that he or she is looking for someone else to fall in love with or to be loved by, it should be no surprise at all that he accepts the person who's nearest to hand.

This is why bosses fall in love with secretaries, women with their bosses. It's not that they have been bowled over by love against their will but that they were, for some reason inside themselves, looking for an experience of love and the longing has fixed on the obviously available person who was already a 'known quantity'.

The answer then is always to ask another question: 'What is he or she looking for that isn't in our relationship?'. None of us has to look for or steal or long for something we already have. And, to reduce it to its basic factor, the quality we look for is always love, or the *knowledge* of being loved. For it's possible to have love and not know we have it.

That's why telling helps. So do all the little ways which say: 'I admire you, I like you, I am right on your side, I want you to be happy.' A partner may well go to your 'best' friend for this if you are not his or her best friend yourself.

Wanting to open someone else's letters, or read them by right, is often thought of as a form of excessive curiosity. But it really goes further than this in the sense that all forms of curiosity are an attempt to have control and to dominate.

In learning, reading, finding things out, we gain control over the world we live in, by knowledge and understanding. We are no longer at the mercy of things unknown.

That's fine. But in curiosity about other people's communications – letters, diaries, bills, 'phone calls – it's a matter of wanting to control *them*, of not being able to bear them having any secrets from us or a personal, independent existence in their own right.

And if all this sounds pretty serious, I mean it to. This wish to dominate appears often in families when teenage children are prevented from having any privacy – their letters opened, their movements constantly checked and so on. But in time they will get out from under this domination and assert their rights as individuals. It's merely a matter of time and growth.

But in marriage one cannot move inevitably into certain rights which have been denied from the beginning. If they are denied, the victim either has to knuckle under or enter into battle to reclaim his or her rights (see point 17).

All one can say about a husband or wife, then, who has a partner who opens letters or demands to see them (which is quite different from just liking to see them when they're offered) is that this is something which should never have been allowed to happen. But if it has, it usually means a terrific urge to dominate which is working at a deeper level.

If you want to tackle it all at this level and stir things up, then get expert help. But if the letter-opening is the only thing that seems disturbing and other rights to privacy are respected, it might be better to counter it by practical means – such as getting first to the post – and *then* why not satisfy the partner's curiosity?

part v Sex

Anyone with a problem about sex tends to be much concerned with how things *ought* to be: 'Surely he shouldn't be impotent at his age?'; 'I know I ought to get satisfaction and pleasure out of his love-making but . . .'; 'Is it wrong of us to enjoy making love in this unusual way? Ought we to stop?'; 'Shouldn't a normal man want to make love more often (or less often) than he does?' – and so on.

By these and similar worries people show how very anxious they are to have a set of rules, as it were, to tell them what is normal or morally right for them to feel and do in the sphere of sexual relations.

Perhaps this is to do with the past history of sexual matters and their strong associations with sin. But, whatever the reason, it does mean that many people, although married, still find it difficult to dissociate sex from ideas of morality.

This not only gives rise to sexual problems in the way of emotional inhibitions, such as frigidity or impotence, but also makes these problems more difficult to overcome when they do arise.

For if you are over-concerned with what it is *right* to feel and what *ought* to be felt, it does rather blind you to considering what you *do* actually feel and to getting an understanding of what your partner might be feeling.

This is why this Part does not set out the rules which you might be looking for, but instead sets out to show you that there are *no* rules. The answers to sexual problems, as in most other marriage problems, will depend entirely on your own feelings and those of your partner. I hope this Part will help you to question and understand what some of those feelings might be.

51 Impotence

Occasional impotence in a man – an inability to have or maintain an erection – is about as common as a headcold. It is not a disease, a weakness, an indication of lack of masculinity or an insult to the woman. It's more in the nature of a symptom – of anxiety, a drop in self-confidence, or perhaps even a head-cold.

But a man naturally finds it difficult to see impotence as a sign of some temporary unease. He is the active partner in sexual intercourse and if he does not have an erection there can *be* no sexual intercourse.

This means that he is apt to load his impotence with a deep sense of failure, which increases his anxiety on the next occasion: 'Will I be able to or won't I?' – which, in turn, makes impotence more likely.

So the main answer to this problem is for the woman to smother any ideas she may have about his not wanting to make love to her or being rejected or having half a man by her side, and take the view that it's a slice of bad luck which can happen to anyone (and does).

Once the man can truly feel that there is no question of failure or blame on either side, then both he and his wife are in a position to figure out together what might be the trouble.

Sometimes he might simply be exhausted by work-worries, or a check on his general health is indicated. Sometimes there might be a nagging worry at the back of his mind that he hasn't been able to talk over or scarcely realizes is there.

If the difficulty persists, then ask the doctor about it.

52 Frigidity

Frigidity seems to cover a multitude of conditions. A wife will describe herself as 'frigid' and ask for help if she finds she is not enjoying love-making, or has never had an orgasm, or does not have an orgasm every time, or if she knows she has a real fear of or distaste for love-making.

A husband will describe his wife as 'frigid' if she does not want to make love every time he wants to, if she does not appear to him to enjoy it or if she seems not to want him sexually at all and either refuses relations altogether or merely 'puts up with' infrequent sexual intercourse.

The lack of satisfaction in a wife is discussed in point 57. As far as the other conditions are concerned, it is vitally important for both partners to realize how much a woman's attitude to sex is bound up with her deepest feelings about being loved and her freedom from irrational fears.

She cannot will herself to discard deeply-buried feelings which she does not even know exist – this is rather like saying to a non-swimmer, caught in a powerful under-tow: 'Why don't you just let yourself go and enjoy the dip?'.

Frigidity, therefore, can very rarely be solved by changes in technique or by any means you can read about in a book. It is nearly always to do with a woman's feelings about sex and most of these are likely to be unconscious.

A husband can undoubtedly influence these feelings by helping her to feel loved and desired by his words and actions, and very often this kind of reassurance, which is often sadly considered unnecessary, can make a world of difference between a woman who is fearful of giving herself and one who longs to do so and is able to.

Where this doesn't seem to help or when a husband is unable to meet this need, then it's best to seek help. This kind of problem can be taken with confidence to some Family Planning Clinics, to your own family doctor, or to a Marriage Guidance Council.

53 Frustration

If you feel frustrated, i.e. that you are not getting enough of something you want very much, your instinct is very likely to a blame the person who's withholding what you want b feel there's something wrong with you to be so much in want or c give it up as a bad job, tell yourself you didn't want it all that much anyway and think about finding satisfaction in some other direction.

But these, although very natural reactions, are more or less ways in which a child deals with frustrations. As an adult you can probably manage a bit better than this, especially as all these childish courses fail to solve the problem in the long run.

One helpful way of dealing with it is to see your sex relations, not as a matter of supply and demand (rather as if the grocer had unfairly failed to deliver your regular order), but as an expression of what's going on in the emotions of the two of you.

All our feelings about giving and taking, loving and being loved, dominating and submitting reveal themselves in sexual behaviour. None too clearly, it's true, but all the signs can be read if you care to look at them.

For example, if there's an underlying resentment in one partner, it will show itself in a disinclination to make love – either as an unconscious way of punishing or because there's too much anger and hurt there to allow room for loving feelings.

If one of you is going through a phase of decreased self-confidence or feelings of inadequacy, it will find expression in sex – either in an increased need for the reassurance of love-making or perhaps in a more aggressive approach.

So if you're feeling frustrated, it would obviously help

if you can figure out whether or not your *need* has increased and to let your partner know how you're feeling. And if it's not you but the other who's complaining of frustration, try not to take it as an accusation against you but as a sign of his or her need for just a bit more confirmation that he or she is loved.

At times, too, you can feel frustrated by the absence or sudden withdrawal of one element of sex relations, especially if this has always been there before. A wife can build up feelings of frustration more readily if the tenderness she needs is not part of the sex relations than if a physical climax is not a part of it.

And a husband may feel frustrated, however frequent the occasions for intercourse and the physical satisfaction involved, by the fact that his wife seems to take no part in it or enjoy it or even belittles his attempts to involve her feelings in the whole thing.

Perhaps you can see, therefore, that frustration in *you* can only be tackled by an understanding of what's gone wrong between *us*. It requires the determination to face difficulties rather than suffering them in silence or pretending they're not there.

The prime necessity for this solution is that both of you should be able to talk to each other about your feelings. Don't get into the habit of expecting your partner to be a mind-reader or believing that sex is 'doing what comes naturally' and therefore doesn't need to be talked about. It does.

54 Frequency of sexual intercourse

Sometimes this is the problem of one partner, if the husband or wife is wanting more or less love-making than the other is happy about.

And sometimes it's a problem they both have, in that they wonder if the number of times they make love is 'normal' or 'right', whether they are not being self-indulgent and possibly harmful to make love so often or whether they are not a bit 'under-sexed' and, by implication, unhealthy to make love so infrequently.

But, as I said in the introduction to this Part, what suits both partners and is agreeable and enjoyable to them both is 'right' for them. Why mar this obviously happy state of affairs by comparing your performance with other people's, or with the mythical Mr. and Mrs. Average?

Where there is disagreement between the partners, it is no

answer for either of them to appeal to any idea of what is 'right' or 'normal' for anyone else.

She may be convinced that it is unnatural for a man to want sexual intercourse every night of the week, but in fact her husband *does*, and this is a measure of sexual desire which is perfectly natural for him.

He, for his part, may accuse his wife of being under-sexed and say that she cannot love him if she does not feel the urge to make love as often as he does. But she does *not* feel the same as he does and this is something they both have to come to terms with and adjust to.

The whole course of marriage is full of similar adjustments, from beginning to end, consisting of constant recognition of what *is*, of the differences between the partners and the need for a little self-control in one direction, a little more generosity in another and a lot of understanding and acceptance flowing in all directions.

The way this works on the subject of the frequency of sexual intercourse is that, whether it continues from the early years at the rate of several times a week or settles down into once a week or less, it matters to no-one else but the couple concerned. They need only harmonize with *each other*, not with any imagined norms or rules.

55 Menstruation

A minor problem connected with menstruation is that some husbands and wives wonder if it is wrong or harmful to have sexual intercourse during the wife's monthly period.

And what often leads to this quandary is the increase in sexual feelings felt by some women during the time of their periods. This is not true of all women, though the majority do have a certain rhythmic pattern in the strength of their sexual feelings – a fact which an observant couple can note and act on to their mutual advantage. Some, for instance, are more sexually-inclined mid-way between periods, some just before and just after, some during a period.

It's clearly all to the good, in the progress towards harmony and mutual enjoyment, for both husband and wife to know what her particular pattern of sexual feeling is. But what if the time when she most feels like love-making is during a period?

All I can say – once more – is that this is up to the husband and wife. Some people have religious objections to any contact between the sexes during a period and presumably there is no question, for people who hold these views, of having intercourse at this time.

For others, it is enough to say that there is nothing morally wrong in it if both partners are agreeable. But many men and women have aesthetic objections to this which are liable to outweigh the pleasurable aspects – after intercourse if not before.

But then again they might not; it's one of those occasions when one needs perhaps to be particularly sensitive to the other person's feelings and do without this particular sex activity if there's the slightest indication of regret or distaste.

A final point worth making is that intercourse during a period is not in any way harmful. And conception is highly improbable but has been known to happen.

56 Is this unnatural?

Few people now consider there is anything reprehensible in experimenting with different positions in sexual intercourse, or indulging in all kinds of erotic play as a preliminary to it.

Where there's disagreement between partners on this score, it's more likely to arise from feelings of inhibition – a reluctance to let go and abandon himself or herself – than from moral considerations. This is something only the partners can overcome in their own way in the process of working out what is agreeable and pleasurable to both of them.

Still, however keen you are to vary your sexual activity, there are some positions which are in fact pretty uncomfortable and offer no pleasure to at least one of the partners. They may be neither indecent nor perverted in themselves (as nothing is which is acceptable to both) but they may be merely tedious or too much like gymnastics.

Some sexual practices have been condemned in the past, either by convention or by law. Buggery, even between husband and wife, is still technically an offence, but it's regarded with far less horror or interest than it used to be and is recognised as something which some husbands and wives enjoy and others don't. It is far too common to be considered a perversion.

So too are cunnilingus and fellatio – both forms of mouth-genital contact which are widely practised as a preliminary to love-making.

Again there is no need to give yourself a problem by wondering if these are 'wrong' or 'unnatural' but, of course, these misgivings might be a cover for the fact that you don't, in truth, find them very pleasurable or acceptable. In which case, it would be better all round if you told your partner what you really felt and adapted to each other's feelings accordingly. But the main point is that there's no need to feel guilty about anything you do, provided it's welcome to both and isn't causing either of you any physical or mental harm (see point 100).

57 Lack of satisfaction

There are far too many good books available on sexual technique for me to say anything here about the kinds of failure to reach a climax, in the woman or, more rarely, in the man, through such physical problems as temporary impotence (see point 51), premature ejaculation, coitus interruptus (see point 58) or lack of enough preliminary stimulation. I have recommended a few of these books in the reading-list at the back.

Knowing what's what about the physical feelings involved can usually overcome a man's problem about a failure to gain satisfaction or a climax (people have different names for it), for this is the natural result of his achieving and completing the sexual act at all.

But it's not so for a woman. She can make love throughout her married life, conceive and bear children without ever having a climax at all. But this doesn't mean that she necessarily has a problem. She may entirely enjoy love-making as much if not more than a woman who experiences orgasms every time as a matter of course. Some wives experience an intense sharing of the husband's climax and feel satisfaction in that way.

But some do feel dissatisfied and deprived by their failure to have an orgasm. One thing not to do is to pretend that all's well and simulate an orgasm for your husband's sake. Apart from bringing 'play-acting' into a situation where this doesn't belong, it gets you nowhere in solving the problem.

If you approach it in the spirit of: 'I wonder what's stopping me from enjoying this as much as I could?', it's not going to hurt his feelings nearly as much as your deception would if he knew of it (and sometimes husbands are only too aware of it).

And what is stopping you? Better rule out first all the very common practical reasons. Fear of conception (see point 58), a lack of privacy or fear of interruption, ignorance about what an orgasm is (how and where it's felt) or not enough leading-up to the sexual act (not all husbands appreciate that a woman's body simply cannot, biologically, warm up from cold to readiness for intercourse in a few seconds flat).

If all these factors have been ruled out or put right and still no joy, you can take it that, for some reason, you're not yet able to relax and give yourself up to love-making in the way that makes an orgasm possible.

This is saying something about *you* and not just about your love-making. Perhaps you tend to lead a rather tense and anxious life all round. Better take a cool look at yourself and see if you can't relax a bit more and let things be instead of wanting to exert too much control over life.

Or perhaps you're trying to keep worries from your husband and yourself which would be lightened by getting them out and talking them over. Or you may notice in yourself enough tension to warrant a visit to your doctor.

Meanwhile, while you are discovering ways of being a more relaxed person, forget about the striving for an orgasm. Relax during love-making too, and tell yourself you're just going to enjoy it and help your husband to enjoy it. And after a while that's how it'll happen.

58 Contraception

There are five methods in current use for the prevention of conception. One, used by the man, is the sheath or French letter. Three, used by the woman, are the famous Pill, the diaphragm and the intra-uterine device (IUD for short).

The fifth, practised by people with religious objections to 'mechanical' contraception, is the natural or rhythm method which means abstaining from sexual intercourse at those times of the month when the wife is most likely to conceive. This has to be worked out by the wife and involves the making of a temperature chart to find out when she is and is not ovulating.

There is also a sixth method, *coitus interruptus*, which means that the husband withdraws from his wife's vagina before he reaches a climax and emits semen. This is so chancey that it can scarcely be called a reliable method of contraception; it can also lead to rather dissatisfied feelings in both partners; nevertheless, some couples prefer it to any other way.

The sheath can be bought over the counter or by post. The methods used by a woman, however, cannot. They need to be prescribed or fitted by a doctor to make sure that they suit the woman personally.

Your own doctor can do this. Or you can go to your local Family Planning Clinic and, for the cost of the appliance and a small fee, you can discuss your contraceptive problems with a woman doctor, be fitted, or prescribed for, with the method of your choice and continue to check with the Clinic its effectiveness and suitability over the years, especially after the birth of your children.

Since this is, rightly, considered a wife's responsibility, there is hardly any problem which she can't sort out with the doctor who's advising her.

But very rarely there will be disagreement between husbands and wives about whether contraception should be practised at all. Behind this are invariably opposite views on when to have the first child, or additional children, or even a conflict about whether they should have children at all.

This is rather a serious problem which can't be answered by the wife taking the matter into her own hands and going ahead with what she wants – either preventing conception or not.

It would therefore be better to get outside help for this problem from your doctor, Family Planning Clinic doctor or marriage guidance counsellor.

59 Sub-fertility

If you have been trying for a baby for a year and have had no success, then it's wise not to put off getting advice about this problem for much longer.

For one thing, many cases of sub-fertility are due to very minor causes which can be put right – such as a change of position in love-making or a watch kept on the best time of the month for conception – and it would be a pity to worry any longer without finding out if you are in this group.

For another thing, if it does turn out that you are unable to have children, you will probably not want to wait too long before coming to a decision about adoption (point 60).

The first step is to see your own doctor. He will be in charge of the tests and any treatment that's necessary, but he will direct you for these tests to a clinic which specializes in doing them.

There is nothing alarming about any of the procedures for finding out what might be wrong, although husbands are naturally a little sheepish about their part in it and wives can be very apprehensive – but these feelings are well-understood by the doctors and nurses who help with this problem. The wife will probably have a simple internal investigation, the husband may be asked to provide a sample of semen, and both will have a check on their general health.

When it's found that a couple is unable to have children, it's not always possible to say why, or which partner is the infertile one — but I don't suppose that this is a vitally important point to a couple who are *both* of them disappointed and want to help each other adapt to the disappointment.

Many Family Planning Clinics also operate a sub-fertility clinic, so that you might, instead, prefer to discuss this problem at a clinic you have already attended for contraceptive help or to find out about a clinic which can help you, if your own cannot.

You can get information about this from the headquarters of the Family Planning Association (see the list of helping agencies in Appendix A).

60 Adoption

Adopting a baby is a very emotional undertaking for the couple who's adopting but the thing to bear in mind is that it's a closely supervised, highly organised undertaking for everyone concerned. So be prepared for lots of discussion and investigation, quite a bit of delay and not getting the blue-eyed boy you'd set your heart on and perhaps having a dark-eyed girl instead.

The rules about adoption are broadly that you should be able to afford to maintain the child reasonably well, that one would-be adopter should be at least 25 and the other 21 (unless they want to adopt a relation), and that they should not be more than 40 years older than the child.

You can find out more about adoption and receive a list of registered adoption societies by writing to The Standing Conference of Adoption Societies (details in Appendix A).

Local authorities also arrange adoptions, so you could approach the county Children's Officer instead.

Some of the adoption societies which are run by different Churches do expect would-be adopters to hold religious beliefs and to bring up the child in accordance with these beliefs. This has led many people to discard the idea of adoption because they feel they cannot qualify on religious grounds. But not all adoption societies have this rule, and some local authorities do not. There is also the Agnostics Adoption Society — which obviously has no religious slant at all — and their address is in Appendix A.

By middle age any worrying problem about sex has usually been overcome or pushed out of sight for ever. But middle age brings some of its own sexual problems, most of them having their source in the emotional changes and re-adaptations which take place in the 40's and 50's.

In the realm of sex, these emotional changes may find expression in an unexpected lack of confidence, perhaps a temporary impotence in the man, a falling-off in desire by the woman.

When she has the change of life, this may affect her in the same way, so that for the time being she loses her response to life generally and can be occasionally irritable, depressed or just out of love with her life and everyone in it.

She can help herself a great deal if this happens, by getting medical help if the symptoms become too trying, by making sure she is what a doctor has described as 'sexually kind', i.e. being loving even when she doesn't feel particularly amorous herself, and by drawing on her own and her family's resources of patience and humour.

What is usually happening in middle age is that you find yourself taking stock of how your life and relationships have been up to then. There's some sadness in this for some people when they note what they have failed to achieve instead of what they have achieved.

This can lead to a re-awakening of old longings for the excitement and magic of an infatuation or for a drastic change in your fortunes. Some women may feel that 'one more baby' is the answer. Some men believe they will recapture their lost purpose and youth by a love-affair or a change of job.

So it's now that the love and understanding you've built up over the years comes into its own. Maybe it has never really been used before in the rush of family life and the feeling that time was on your side. But now it needs to be.

And it's often not until middle age that a husband and wife are able to confront each other as real people and see how their love has weathered all kinds of ups and downs. Many say that their sex-life is 'better than it's ever been' and that what it loses in quantity, it gains in quality.

Some couples in late middle age wonder if it's harmful to continue to enjoy intercourse into the 60's and 70's. Well, the medical opinion is that no physical harm can possibly result from having sex as long as it's possible and enjoyable, but that it's obviously wise to stop short at any sign of strain.

A woman's fertility usually begins to decrease after the early forties, but it is possible for her to conceive until after the menopause is complete. If a contraceptive is being used, the general opinion is that it's safe to do without it when there has been no period for a complete year. There is no such final stop, however, in a man's fertility. He can remain both potent and fertile into his 70's and later.

For some useful reading-matter on middle age, consult the reading-list in Appendix B.

part vi The Family

When the family starts increasing, then we take on new roles as parents and begin to form new relationships, mother to son, father to daughter, wife-mother to husband-father and so on. It's rather different from the old straight 'you and me' as man and woman. We gain a lot and give up quite a lot too. This chapter is about these changes in your marriage and some of the problems they can bring.

62 Worries of the mother-to-be

Any practical problems the mother-to-be might have can very simply be solved by asking her doctor, raising the point at the clinic or consulting one of the large number of books on pregnancy (see '101 Facts an Expectant Mother should know' in Appendix B).

But sometimes her pregnancy brings emotional problems to the marriage. A wife's sexual feelings, which are so closely bound up with having babies and feeding them, may appear to her husband to have cooled towards him. So he does need at this time to feel he's a part of the whole process and not left out in the cold now that his contribution has been made!

Unless advised otherwise by your doctor, you can safely continue to make love until six weeks before the baby's due. Women with a history of miscarriage are often cautioned to avoid sex relations (and any other vigorous activity) at the times their periods would normally fall.

Even then, if intercourse itself is contra-indicated or not welcome, there are all kinds of other ways in which a wife can continue to show her love and make her husband feel wanted and happy.

For some women their pregnancy gives them a feeling of liberation and well-being which actually makes sex relations more enjoyable than before. It is often, then, the husband who may be a little fearful of harming his wife or the expected baby. This is a common fear and can be put right either by a wife's reassurance or by a word with the doctor.

There may also be fear on the part of the woman – a fear of childbirth as being dangerous or even fatal, or a fear that she is not 'maternal' enough to care for her baby properly. Both these fears, amounting almost to panic in some women, are well-recognised by doctors and can be helped.

So it's most important that, if you have such fears, you don't keep them buried and fret away silently but are prepared to tell your husband and doctor and get them alleviated.

The happiest babies are those born to confident, happy mothers – and there's no reason why, with the right help when it's needed, any woman can't be just the kind of person her baby needs her to be.

63 Worries of the father-to-be

Fathers-to-be sometimes feel rather hard done by. After all, they have the expense, the responsibility, the care and the protection of the mother to worry about. All the wife has to do is have the baby!

If he has particularly needed the 'motherly' kind of attentions his wife gives him, he can be quite worried about the fact that there will soon be someone else to share these attentions. Already, perhaps, his wife is a little withdrawn into herself, going about the house with a secret air of expectancy about her and spending a lot of hours nest-building.

So it's not always easy for a man to welcome the pregnancy as much as his wife wants him to. He may even feel a little surprised with himself for not feeling all that excited about the coming baby. But there's nothing surprising about this. It's difficult for a man to visualise a baby before it's there, as a woman can, and it's quite impossible for him to feel paternal about what is, after all, a non-person as yet.

If there are any upsets, therefore, about attitudes to the expected baby –'You don't seem to be in the least interested' from her, or from him, 'All you seem to think about is someone who's not even here yet . . .' – it's helpful to realise just how different are the feelings of the two sexes about this and how fruitless it is to attempt to make your partner feel the same way as you do.

There are also some fathers-to-be, like some mothers-to-be, who deep down are frightened or unwilling to be parents. They may get extremely worried before the baby comes and feel very guilty about not being overjoyed and full of smiles like their friends in the same position.

If this is the case, then it's a good idea to talk it over with an expert – a doctor or marriage guidance counsellor – so that being a father can be the delight for you that it is for others.

Well, yes, there are mixed feelings – even if you don't always want to know about them. But knowing about them helps to prevent them becoming problems.

The baby's there and everything's fine – it's 'the three of us' now – but why does your husband get so touchy when you get up from the dinner-table because the baby's crying? What makes you feel now and again, to your horror, like giving your infant son a slap instead of the cuddle he wants?

And why doesn't he lie contentedly in your arms instead of screaming his head off – could it be that he doesn't love you? Or that you're doing something wrong? And is it right that already you should be just a bit bored with all the bathing, nappy-washing and pram-wheeling?

So it isn't roses all the way. A husband can feel jealous of the baby; a wife can feel tired and too much in demand; she can feel fed-up and depressed soon after the baby's born (but should tell her doctor about it if it's persistent or more intense than a feeling of low-spiritedness over a period of a few days). None of these feelings is anything to be alarmed about, or to need more than just *having* the feelings until they pass. As they will.

Every mother knows that later on, when the children are older, the occasional feelings of irritation with them, the exasperation and anger, all go along with the basic feeling of loving them and not wanting them to be any other way than they are – their unique, interesting (and maddening) selves!

But this mixture of feelings, so easily recognisable when the children are less dependent on us, are also there when the baby is little. It's part of having feelings at all and is the opposite of indifference or of having no real feelings (see point 39).

In a few months you'll be able to see that your baby also has this mixture of feelings. He gets angry with you (and he won't just be able to feel it, as you can; he'll have to show it, by his kicking and face-pulling and yelling).

If you've already come to realise that love is mixed up with these and similar negative feelings, then you won't be in the least worried or hurt by them. A wise, and very warm book about this whole subject, which you might like to read, is Dr D. Winnicott's 'The Child, The Family and the Outside World.' Penguin Books 4s 6d.

65 'She's no longer my wife'

This is how a husband can feel if all the attention is given to the baby, and his wife's tiredness and disinclination to make love, or perhaps even her failure to notice him at all (if this is what it looks like to him) just gets too much for him.

Everything is so different, so geared to the newcomer, that it feels to him that the wife he used to have has changed places with a mother.

Well, one thing to come to terms with is that being a parent does require some sacrifices of our own needs. Mothers give up going out so much and having those dressed-up occasions which women enjoy; or they give up their jobs for a while and work much harder at home instead.

They enjoy it mostly, but it *is* different and it takes time to appreciate the new pleasures which have replaced the old ones.

So both parents are facing this re-adaptation from the two-person relationship to a family-centred one and, while they are getting re-orientated, both are likely to feel they have lost *something*. It may be freedom, exclusive attention from each other, evenings out together or uninterrupted nights.

For the mother, with her close, rewarding relationship with the baby, there are more occasions for appreciating all that's been gained by these changes.

For the father, the rewards come later when the baby needs him too. Meanwhile, he's doing his best for the baby if he can help his wife to feel loved and protected and therefore able to handle the baby in an unanxious, confident way.

66 'He doesn't seem to realise he's a father now'

When a wife complains that her husband 'takes no interest in the baby', or spends as much on his car as he used to in the pre-baby days or still wants to have a pint with his friends (or more pints perhaps since she's got the 6 o'clock feed to cope with before starting the evening meal), she's really only saying 'why doesn't he feel like I do?'

But, of course, he can't. He's not a mother. And he won't realise he's a father until the baby is old enough to respond a little and make him *feel* like a father. If you try to force him into being a parent before he's ready, then the whole marvellous business of having a family is going to drive you apart instead of bringing you closer together. So don't force him, or try to make him have your feelings.

Some men, on the other hand, are more than usually identified with the mother's role and are very keen to share in the mother's duties, even to the extent of making her feel inadequate in the way she does them on her own.

I'm sure you won't refuse his help or opinions, but if it looks as if he can't let you get on with the job, and makes you feel on edge and anxious about the way you're handling things, it would certainly help to discuss this with your doctor or health visitor.

But fathers do take a much more active share in caring for the baby now, and it's not likely that this will upset the harmony in the home at all unless the wife is already unsure of herself and in need of help for her own sake.

67 The grandparents

It's funny how what *your* parents do can feel like friendly interest and what your in-laws do feels like interference! In other words, any problem about grandparents has less to do with what their real attitude to the baby is than how you feel about it. So that's the way you'd better tackle it, by looking at the feelings involved rather than the actions.

Let's see how this works. When your mother or his mother says: 'Do you really think it's best to leave him in the pram in this bitter weather?' you can take it in one of two ways.

If you're a bit unsure of yourself, or are not overfond of the questioner, you may at once take this as a criticism. She seems to be saying: 'It's not best to leave him in the pram and you're a rotten mother'.

If, on the other hand, you're not looking for trouble or expecting criticism, you can take it that what's behind the question is: 'Methods of baby-care are so different from my day; I wonder if it's considered healthy to have them out in all weathers?' The response to this reading of the message might be: 'Well, they say it's good for the baby provided he's wrapped up warm and out of the wind. Was it different when you had me (or John)? Tell me what you did'.

Grandparents who are forever offering advice don't have to be taken as opposition. A lot of your feelings will depend on how you saw your own parents when you were little – as interested supporters, allowing you your own views, or as authoritarian figures who undermined your confidence. If it was the latter, you need to beware of putting this child's eye view onto your parents and onto the other set of grandparents now. It's past history and you're a big girl now.

When they offer advice you don't agree with, it's really quite easy to take it as well meant and as an expression of an interesting point of view which is not necessarily yours too: 'Oh really, is that the way you used to do it? I like to do it this way', and do it your way.

A really 'bossy' grandparent, who's constantly advising, may often be doing so because you've never *asked* for advice or help, and this is the only way they can express their natural interest and love of a grandchild.

It's really very easy to make a grandparent feel he or she's contributing by asking for her view on small matters: 'Does it look to you as if he's teething?' – a view you can accept but don't have to adopt.

And the more you ask and draw them in, the less they'll have to keep testing their welcome and forcing their concern on you by unwanted advice.

68 That tied-down feeling

This is a feeling that invariably passes, by the very nature of being parents. But it may linger in the wife, especially if her husband has solved the problem in his way, by using the greater freedom from the home he undoubtedly has and leaving his wife to experience the tied-down feeling on her own.

The answer here is that, like it or not, a husband must try to see how imprisoned by her own emotions a wife can get to feel. It is not always that the ironing *must* be done before they can go out, that this baby-sitter and that baby-sitter is actually unsuitable.

Mostly it is that, in her drive to be a good wife, housekeeper and mother, she cannot enjoy herself with the ironing left undone at home or with a sitter-in who, she feels, might do the wrong thing when the baby wakes.

A husband cannot wrench his wife out of this self-imprisonment by insisting she comes out 'for her own good'. Invariably he will give up trying and will more and more find his own diversions.

So his wife feels more tied-down and ends up with what she was unconsciously seeking at the very beginning – the feeling of being entirely responsible for running the family and being taken for granted as chief slave and bottle-washer.

This is something which has to be tackled early – it's difficult to retrieve when past a certain point. You, as a husband, may see a big difference in your wife's heaping up of troubles for herself if you switch from trying to make her come out 'for her sake' and ask her to come out for yours. 'I want you with me', 'I'd much rather have this evening out than all the ironing done; I'll do my shirt in the morning'.

You, as a wife, may find it not too difficult to let go of the more unnecessary reins if you stop to consider how much of your 'tied-down feeling' is self-imposed.

What actually happens if you take up mother's offer to have the baby there for the night while you and your husband go to the theatre? What are the results if you leave the room uncleaned and get sunk in a library book instead? If you go and see a friend one evening and leave your husband to sit-in and get his own evening meal?

The only way to find out is to do it. And what you'll find, to your growing delight, is that being tied-down is never a reality, only an attitude of mind. We are all only as free as we mean to be.

69 Disagreements on upbringing

We've all been 'brought up' in one way or another and since this process took place in our formative years, and involved the people we had strong feelings about at the time, we can't fail to be enormously influenced by the way this was done.

So we bring ourselves and our deepest feelings into the matter of bringing up our own children. For this reason some disagreements are inevitable.

Perhaps both parents had a strict upbringing and feel they have this in common. But one may have felt secure in this strictness and have taken strength from it. He or she will feel that discipline is a good thing for the children.

The other partner may have felt overpowered and threatened by his parents' strictness and has ever since had a struggle to break away from it and be a free person in his own right.

For this parent it will seem very important that the children should have the freedom to be themselves, to have rules explained to and accepted by them, to let them have a measure of personal responsibility as soon as it's possible.

What do you do about these disagreements? Well, the only thing is to thrash them out at the talking level long before they get to the stage of action.

If you find yourself administering the odd slap to a child and your husband feels pretty strongly that this is a bad thing, or the other way round, it can do nothing but good for you both to consider why you're slapping, why he doesn't, what you both think slapping actually does (for you and the child) and even find out what other people think about it.

Apart from being a fascinating subject, our views about bringing up children reveal to others and to ourselves an interesting side-light on our attitudes to life – in fact, they are the essence of the way we look at life and other people.

So have your disagreements. Air them. Find out what lies behind them. Be vitally interested, if you possibly can, in the 'whys' and 'wherefores' of your own views and your partner's. But not in front of the children, naturally.

With a deeper understanding of the feelings behind each other's views on such things as politeness, punishment, and discipline, there will be chances to modify some views, and a willingness to hold back sometimes from acting on them.

70 Spoiling

Perhaps father invariably gives way when the children plead to stay up 'just a bit longer'. Perhaps mother seems to do too much running about after the children, doing for them little tasks which father feels they ought to be doing for themselves. Or one of you seems to be more indulgent to one child than another. Or a toddler is thought to be fussed and cuddled more than the other parent thinks is necessary or good for him.

Well, you cannot argue with another person's *need* to behave in these ways. If a father habitually comes home with expensive presents for his son or daughter, this is not something you can rationally sort out on the basis of the possible effect on the children.

It does not *have* a rational basis. He buys the presents because he needs to. She cuddles her son a great deal, not because he specially needs the cuddling, but because she does. She continues to do unnecessary things for the children not because she really believes they are dependent on her for these things but because she needs them to stay dependent on her.

And so on. It's illuminating as well as helpful to begin to recognise how much of what a partner does, and of what we ourselves do, springs not from external factors and the needs of others but from needs inside *us*.

No problem about spoiling or any other aspect of family life can be tackled successfully *without* getting some understanding of what our needs are. And once they're understood, it's comparatively easy to help them to be satisfied in other ways.

A husband, for example, may be compelled to give presents in order to feel that he's a generous, loving parent. He may need to confirm this idea of himself over and over again because his own father, whom he admired, was like this or because his father was the opposite and he fears to be like him.

Yet, once you both get an inkling of these needs, it is not so hard for him to see that they can be met in ways that are more constructive for the children – such as giving them listening-time instead of material presents, or showing them how to mend old toys instead of providing them with new.

In this way, the 'spoiling' parent might even be able to give up this need to over-indulge and be prepared to be himself or herself, alert to give comfort and cuddling when the child clearly needs it (and their signals are always *very* clear), but no longer so anxious to anticipate the child's every want or to mistake the parents' own needs for those of the child.

71 Punishments and rewards

How you feel about these things will depend on your basic views on the rearing of children (see point 69). Someone who believes in firm discipline is likely to believe also in the principle of punishment (tho' not necessarily of reward) since clearly one cannot impose discipline without a built-in threat of what happens if the rules aren't obeyed.

Other parents who tend more towards self-expression and the building-up in the child of inner rules based on his own feelings about people may be very much against punishment and reward.

Where there is confidence in both partners about either of these ways, there's no problem. (I except, of course, the kind of corporal punishment which amounts to cruelty. If you have the slightest suspicion that you or your partner is punishing in a way that could damage a child, mentally or physically, you *must* take these worries to your doctor or the local Children's Officer.)

But all parents come to perceive that children often seek out punishment, or need to come up against an unyielding, firm stand against their own impulses.

We can see this when a child goes on and on with some tormenting form of naughtiness until we lose patience and round on him with: 'And now you've gone too far. You'll have to go to your room, (or miss television or whatever your form of punishment is). You asked for it . . .'. And indeed he did.

Not to go too deeply into psychology, the experts have ample proof that children have inborn feelings of guilt. These may have no cause in his real everyday life, but they make it necessary for him now and again to manoeuvre himself into being punished.

This relieves his guilt and undoes the wrong feeling; for now he has paid for it and been forgiven and the way is open to feel good and right again.

Without any rules, no boundaries between right and wrong, no punishments, he can very well be all at sea with his guilt-feelings and fear that he can 'get away with murder' and no one will stop him. Some rules therefore, some limits to your tolerance and some form of punishment, represent to a child safety and love.

Problems about punishment and reward will, I hope, seem a lot easier if you think about this and work out how it may apply to your child and your way of bringing him up.

72 Hopes and fears

We all have hopes and fears about our children, some of them are obvious – that they will be healthy and happy – and some of them are hidden – that they will be artistic (like us) or she will be a ballet-dancer (because you wanted to be but couldn't) or that he will be a Prime Minister (because Lloyd George knew your father).

Problems only arise here when the hopes and fears are inordinate and interfere with your ability to let a child be himself and choose the direction that suits his nature and talents rather than your longings.

This means, of course, that he or she has to be given a wide range of directions to choose from. It's here that sometimes we unconsciously narrow his choice by simply leaving out the opportunities which don't count with us, are disapproved of or 'aren't what we had in mind'.

We may discourage, for example, an interest in the kind of reading which does not interest us. 'Oh, that's just about aeroplanes. It wouldn't appeal to you'. Or in other activities: 'How on earth can you want to go swimming on a day like this – it will be much too cold'. (Too cold for him, or too cold for you?) Underlying this is the aim to make him feel like us, rather than the hope that he will be, and feel for, himself.

If these hopes are too strong, extending to a pretty severe domination of the child's thinking and feeling, the results may not be apparent until much later – in an adolescent who either 'has no mind of his own' or one who can only be himself by defying other people, perhaps with violence (see point 73).

All in all, hopes and fears are no problem if they're not too limited. To hope that he'll be happy, to fear that he'll have more unhappiness than he can cope with (for you can't realistically hope that he'll never be unhappy) – these are about the only ones broad enough to let your child grow up with his own hopes and fears rather than yours.

73 The problem child

If it ever gets to the stage that your child is a problem – not just the source of problems now and again – then you need help and should get it.

The only yardstick for recognising when help is needed is when you feel you need it and can't cope any longer without it. This may range from school truancy to bed-wetting, from teenage delinquency to nightmares.

Your doctor is the first person to go to with the problem. Let him decide whether it's a physical or mental problem (or both). If it's primarily a psychological problem he may refer you to the nearest Child Guidance Clinic. Some clinics also have an Adolescent Unit, or your doctor will know of other sources of help.

Referral to a Child Guidance Clinic may also come from a headmaster or headmistress. So, if your child's problem presents itself mainly at school, you may like to talk it over first with the school principal.

There are other groups of parents who face unique problems. These are the parents of children who are handicapped, either physically or mentally or both.

There is now a great deal of help available for these parents from organisations which exist to help people in these circumstances to co-operate with each other and to spread the word about facilities and practical help available.

There is a list of these organisations and helpful guidance in a booklet called 'Parents under Stress' by Dr T. A. Ratcliffe and Angela Reed. Details in Appendix B.

74 Sex and the children

I think those 'little talks' between father and son or mother and daughter are a little old hat now. Most of us realise that the time to give the facts is when a child's ready for them – that is, when he or she asks.

Most often he or she will ask mother, because she's more part of everyday life and this is how, left to himself, the child will approach sex – as an interesting part of everyday life.

How to answer? With what words? How much or how little to explain in one go? How to get the feelings across as well as the facts?

Well a lot of this will depend on what sort of person you are (for that is teaching him a lot about love and sex) and on what kind of relationship you and your partner have (and that will tell him almost everything about relationships). So this is in your hands entirely. But there's a helping hand in the numerous booklets on this subject, for you or your children to read. You'll find some suggestions and details in Appendix B.

75 Favouritism

Left to itself it's very doubtful that favouritism can actually harm the favoured child. The unfavoured ones may feel intensely envious and competitive, but most children feel like that anyway, however fair and just the parents are.

It can be a problem, however, to the parent who's not doing the favouring. If father seems to dote on one child for instance, it's mother who may resent this far more than any of the other children do.

Even then, it need be no problem if she can see these feelings and recognise them as natural and a bit childish and thus make doubly sure she doesn't whip up similar feelings in the other children.

But favouritism is really an inevitable part of family life. We may have the ideal of 'treating all of them the same'. But we know that they are not the same and to answer the individual need of each child will mean that one child has more of *something* than another.

One has more reassurance because he is less confident; one has more encouragement because he has more fear of failure; one has more freedom because he is more responsible, and so on.

There is a problem with the eldest. He or she may seem to be favoured with more material things simply because the younger ones get the reach-me-downs and the older one gets them new. He gets the new bike and Number Two gets the one the eldest has outgrown.

But, in truth, children will set as much store by the newness and cash price of objects as we do ourselves, no more and no less. Perhaps they can be helped to see that love is not the new coat or the expensive watch. If it comes to them, instead, in the form of the answers to their own emotional needs, they won't feel either unduly favoured or unfavoured.

76 Problems with the adolescent

The one barrier to coping successfully with the ups and downs of adolescence seems to be that some parents take the whole battle *personally*.

They get upset when father and teenage son have bitter arguments about politics, or when mother and daughter fall out over the pig-sty she calls 'her room'.

But we most of us know that growing-up is a process of breaking away from received ideas about life and the self and finding our own identity. And what else have our children to break away from, except us?

So, of course, they'll swing as far in the opposite direction as they can in order to take a detached look at us and what we stand for.

If you're rather religious it's almost a necessity for your son or daughter to go through an atheist stage before he can make up his mind for himself. He may come back to being a firm believer but it won't be his own belief until he's first had a go at discarding it.

We have to let all this happen. If we make noises about wanting respect and gratitude (which would be very nice, but they're not in the parent-child contract) or get hurt, disappointed or angry about their aggressive ways of becoming independent, then we make growing-up that much more painful and difficult for them and us.

When your teenage daughter slams the door and withdraws to her room she is not saying 'I don't want you' but rather 'I don't want authority, protection, childhood, commands and orders. I want to be me.' But who is she? That's what it's all about – and we can only stand staunchly on the side-lines while she finds out.

If there are more serious behaviour problems, however, you may feel you need help. I've mentioned that some Child Guidance Clinics have an Adolescent Unit. Your doctor is the person to ask about this. There are also young people's consultation centres in some cities, where they can go to talk over their problems with a social worker or psychiatrist. Marriage guidance counsellors will also help anyone with a problem concerning their adolescent children.

part vii Common Complaints

I call these problems 'complaints' not because you, the suffering partner on the receiving end of them, complains about them (although, of course, you do!) but because they are so often a 'complaint' for your partner, a symptom of some other unease.

Let's take the analogy of physical problems. If you have a continual headache, or a twitch or a sore foot – a physical complaint – then you think: 'I wonder what this means? There's obviously something not quite right with me in some way. I'd better find out. I'll go and see the doc'.

You tell the doctor about your complaint; he finds what this symptom indicates and you get treatment for the *causes* of the sore foot, headache or whatever.

All through this process there is no question of your wife or husband blaming you for the sore foot or headache. He or she certainly doesn't take the line: 'Look what your headache is doing to me! How can you treat me so badly? How can you expect me to put up with it? Why did I marry someone who has headaches?'

Yet this is often how we behave when the complaint is emotional and not physical – when there is an evident compulsion to spend recklessly, or hang on to money, or the partner becomes bored, clinging or trapped.

But the only answer is to look at it in the other way, as with physical problems, and look for causes. For if you are only concerned with the effect on you, the next step is to see the complaint as something sent to try you or even deliberately inflicted on you by the ill-will of your partner. Then battle is joined and the problem will never be solved – it will just escalate.

It's not easy to ask 'why?' when you're feeling rather wronged and are fed-up with the extravagance or irresponsibility of your partner. But it's not all that difficult either, once you can say to yourself: 'Well, the way he's behaving is a problem for me. But perhaps it's a problem for him too; maybe a bigger one. How does he feel about it? Why does he do these things? If I had an idea of his feelings, perhaps I could understand, and perhaps it would make things a bit better for both of us . . .'.

The very act of asking 'why?' is a loving thing to do. You don't even, at this stage, need to ask him or her. If communications are a little strained, this might be too difficult at the moment.

But you can certainly ask yourself and start the process of understanding why he or she has this 'complaint'. This Part is to help you to do this.

77 The extravagant partner

Extravagance is a relative thing and one of the first things to do, if you feel a partner is spending more than he or she should, is to make sure that your notion of extravagance isn't too much out of line with reality.

Perhaps you can remember that as a child you might have been called extravagant or been accused of wasting your money if you spent it in one fell swoop on something you wanted very much but which seemed quite valueless and 'rubbishy' to everyone else.

It was immaterial to your elders that you had the money and could afford what you bought. To them it was a waste, because what you bought was not something *they* valued.

We cannot help feeling like this sometimes with our own children, or about the spending-habits of other people we know. How extravagant they seem if they buy a caravan when they can't afford carpets! And, because we put carpets before caravans in our list of priorities, it's hard to see that they might put them the other way round.

In a marriage, these differences in our wishes and feelings about priorities in spending become even more obvious. Even if we don't talk about them – and it would all be a lot easier if we did – they stick out like a sore thumb every time one partner feels aggrieved by the spending of the other on something he thought important or necessary.

And this looks awfully like extravagance to the one who can't see either the necessity or the importance.

So we need to talk a lot more about money, and spending, and the wants and emotions that lie behind it. Budgeting is not just a way of working out pounds, shillings and pence; it's a compromise between two people's feelings about what's important to them (see point 32).

If you've reached the stage of just not being able to talk about money because you are too angry about the other's extravagance or meanness, or because you're ground down by money muddles and debts, then you probably need help. One of the agencies in Appendix A could be approached for this.

78 The mean partner

A tight hold on the money-bags usually goes with a tight hold on most other things too. It isn't a characteristic we care for at all in ourselves or other people – whereas extravagance can be seen as a more attractive attitude to life in general.

So you can be sure that if your partner is keeping this tight control over money and possessions, and probably over his feelings too, he's none too happy about it and deep down wishes he were otherwise.

So what's behind it? Of course, there are always some practical reasons. Maybe you really *are* hard up and a cautious eye needs to be kept on the spending. But if that's the reality, why does this caution come over to you as meanness? These are the kinds of questions it might be helpful to ask yourself.

And if the meanness is not the way you see his caution, but the way he really *is*, and in other ways too (as in a reluctance to share his feelings or a witholding of affection), it would be a step forward for you to try to understand what makes him like this.

For, on the whole, mean people are unhappy people. They are hanging tightly onto what they have because they are afraid of losing it, or of not getting more if that goes.

Deep down it is love and security they are trying to keep such a tight hold on. Because they cannot feel that what they have of these things is enough, they are unable to give them to others. They can't let go and be loving and generous without first feeling loved and safe. So you know the answer – love him, or her.

79 The martyr

The trouble about feeling 'put-upon' and ill-used is that it's rather a comfortable feeling if we're honest about it. It might start with indignation: 'He's not going to get away with walking all over me like that' – but it very soon builds up into: 'I *am* being walked all over. Isn't it terrible? See how I suffer!'

How to break out of this? Well, in the first place you may not want to and your partner may not want you to, at heart. For, while you allow him to walk all over you, he's getting the best end of the deal (apart from his guilty feelings about your suffering, but then they might have become comfortable to him too).

But, whichever end of the deal you're at, you evidently feel that this way of relating to each other isn't a very satisfactory one (otherwise you wouldn't be reading about this problem).

And, of course, we can't pretend that it's a good model for the children to have a mother or father who's taken on the role of martyr. One thing, as you've found, is that it drives out love or any idea that the marriage partners are whole, equal people.

So you might as well assume that it's better if you did something about it. If you're the martyred one, you need to get the idea that your wishes *are* important and that you'd be a great deal happier if you stood up for them now and again instead of letting them be denied, and then saying: 'I wuz robbed'.

There isn't so much to do that you can't, for example, go to an evening class – *if you really want to*. And the point is that you would be a happier person going to the evening class than acting as if you were prevented from going.

Maybe people do make demands on you, but they won't overload you with demands if you draw the line at what you'll meet and what you won't meet (see point 5).

If it's your turn to have the biggest slice of cake, have it. Don't hand it to someone else and then wallow in the idea that no one cares whether you want it or not. How can anyone care about someone who hasn't a care for her own position?

If it's your partner who's the martyr, it's a bit more difficult, for you have an obvious advantage in living alongside a doormat. But I expect you sometimes get the feeling that it would be better to be married to a *person*, someone with ideas of her own, who could have a good laugh about difficulties and who stimulated you to mind about her instead of saying: 'Don't mind me . . .'.

If he or she is forever virtually saying: 'Pardon me for living', you can be pretty sure that living isn't basically much fun for her. You may feel this is largely her fault, but she still needs the kind of jolt that will force her to take a stand that is not a martyred one.

You know what her wants really are; don't let her act as if she hasn't any. Do all in your power to get her on that holiday, out for a visit, or into the shop that sells the washing-machine she wants. (Don't worry; the martyr never wants anything you can't afford.) Most of all, if you love her, show it. Martyrs have all the wind taken out of their sails by *any* appreciation and affection.

It's little use to a woman who feels imprisoned to point out to her that there are no locks on the doors, no bars on the windows and no ever-present jailer. For a well-understood part of this whole feeling of being shut-in and confined to a narrow world is the belief that it is external circumstances and other people who put her and keep her in that situation.

None of us likes to acknowledge that an unsatisfactory way of living might come from inside *us*. Nevertheless this is the only way in which it can be overcome.

For if you insist that it is your husband, or marriage or the children, who are imprisoning you, then you are logically going to wait until they set you free – which means that you will be your own jailer for ever.

So you must try to open a few doors for yourself, as other women do. You have the enormous advantage, unlike most men, of being your own master and doing your work in your own time. You can do twice as much one day and leave all but the essentials the next. You don't have to be a clock-watcher or a sink-hugger – you can go out when it's fine and work when it's wet.

You can take the children with you to more places than you realise. If you want a day without them – and why not? – there's no reason why you and another mother shouldn't get together and you mind her children for a day, along with your own, and, another day, she has yours. If you long for a day nursery, you could even organise one – lots of mothers have (see Appendix A for details).

Above all, you need to get rid of the idea that there are any real limits to your world. There is lack of money, not enough time, there are the needs of your husband, home and children. But for many women these are not limitations; they are simply accepted as *being there*, the basic realities of their lives from which all the other possibilities spring.

Remember what Richard Lovelace wrote: 'Stone walls do not a prison make, nor iron bars a cage'. The prisoner he had in mind was *really* in a prison, yet he was free because he had an inner freedom of his own. And you have put iron bars and stone walls around yourself. It's a state of mind.

I hope you can alter it – for no one else can. But others can help you. Your husband, if you can explain how you feel without blaming him, will undoubtedly want to help – for most of us want to love people who are at liberty rather than share a prison sentence.

81 'I'm taken for granted'

What this really means is that your partner – and probably the children too – don't *notice* you anymore. The things you do and say have lost their impact. You get no reaction.

It makes you feel sometimes as if you *weren't there*. You may even get the idea that if you walked into the kitchen with no clothes on, daubed all over with blue woad, they'd only look through you and say: 'What's for supper?'.

One answer is that it's not such a dreadful thing to be so utterly accepted in one role – as home-maker or mother, say – that you are completely relied on to fulfil it consistently and people don't know it's being done.

We really can't expect appreciation and applause for doing these jobs well, any more than a husband gets a pat on the back every day for earning the bread and butter.

Gratitude is nice. But a wife and mother would be rather unrealistic to expect it for the everyday things which represent the basic security and routine of the family.

She can teach the family to say: 'Thank you, that was lovely' at the end of every meal. But she's not teaching them to be grateful. She's only training them to say: 'Thank you, that was lovely'.

All in all, then, being 'taken for granted' in some ways is a measure of your unobtrusive success in meeting the basic needs of the family.

But if this feeling extends to your whole life and you feel: 'I might just as well be a piece of furniture', then clearly you aren't getting any feedback from your loved ones or you aren't giving them anything to feed back *to* you.

If it's that you're actually vital and interesting and amusing but no one else seems to notice this, comment on it or wax appreciative, the usual answer is that you don't go in for this sort of noticing yourself.

This is a kind of currency which either *is* in use in a family or it isn't. If you start using it – noticing the thoughtfulness of others (not necessarily for you!), appreciating a job well done or a new tie, you'll put the coinage into use and some of it will come your way.

The other alternative is that you're not getting feedback because you *are* a bit like a piece of furniture.

Maybe you need to become more interested before you can be interesting – which means looking beyond the kitchen walls and working up enthusiasm for something new and different which will 'take you out of yourself'.

For no one can do this for you. Perhaps you'll learn something, or join a society or take up transcendental meditation. *You* choose.

Or it may be that you are really low and depressed and the greyness inside you is being projected onto the outside world. *They* seem to be taking you for granted because you are taking yourself for granted, as a failure or inadequate. If this is something more than you can struggle out of on your own, then ask your doctor for help.

82 Boredom

A certain occasional boredom with husband or wife or with 'being married' is inevitable. A marriage, after all, lasts a very long time – forty years or more – and it can't be exciting and interesting all the time.

It has its flat patches when we imagine that some other partner or some other way of life might have yielded something more of what we dream of – whether it's romance or luxury or emotional warmth.

It's not treachery to think in this way at times. There is no need to fight the feeling and pretend it's not there. Better to admit to yourself: 'I am bored' and look for ways to involve yourself in something which leaves no room for boredom.

It may be that you've allowed your life to become too monotonous and routine. This is a very easy thing to do in our struggle to maintain shape and order in our lives. It makes us feel safer somehow.

The only way to counteract this is to be brave and tolerate a little disorder – a sudden change of plan when the sun comes out, a reversal of priorities (spend the Christmas savings on a summer holiday instead), or that familiar but well-tried standby, a bold change of hair-style or colour. It's not such a wet idea if you've ever tried it. You might hate it, but you won't be bored.

A total boredom with your husband or wife can only come about if you have relied totally on him or her to provide the interest in your life (see point 85). If you have no reserves of your own – I don't mean necessarily a job of your own or your own circle of friends – it's natural that you would look to him to import whatever points of view are expressed in your marriage. He's seen as the provider of life and you're very much dependent on his moods, his presence and even his wishes.

Well, this can get boring – mainly because another person

cannot indefinitely fill up the vacuum which is inside you.

Your boredom, therefore, is a boredom with yourself. There is no inner zest for life which keeps you going as a person in your own right. Like a child who complains of boredom, you need starting off on a project that becomes your own way of being interested (and interesting) and no one else's.

We open doors for children, but grown-ups have to open their own doors. So dig in your mind for anything which once made you say: 'I'll do that one day' or 'I'll find out all about that when I've got the time'. If you're bored, you've *got* the time. Do it now.

83 'We don't seem to make love any more'

This may be part of a cold war when both of you, for various reasons, want to withdraw from intimacy and deprive each other of sex relations (see point 27).

When one partner begins to feel unhappy about this state of affairs but is unable to restore the closeness, or doesn't know how to, then it's best to get help from doctor or counsellor.

But it may be that you are both fairly satisfied with this state of affairs and are only inclined to think it is 'not right somehow' because of your understanding that sex relations are considered vitally important to mental health and a complete relationship.

But we do not all put the same importance on physical relations. Some husbands and wives may never have obtained a great degree of 'freedom' and satisfaction from physical expressions of love. They may have less sex-drive than others – we all vary. And they may, without loss of love for each other, have spontaneously let sex relations become infrequent or non-existent.

If there is no bitterness about this and no real wish on either side to have things different, there's no need to feel ashamed or compelled to revive something that has no importance for you both.

Sex relations are not obligatory – they are a response to each other. And what you feel for each other may be adequately expressed in other ways which suit you both.

When it doesn't suit you both: 'We don't seem to make love anymore, but I wish we did', then the first answer is to find out why you don't. Part V will help you with this enquiry into what might be the trouble.

84 Irresponsibility

If your problem is that your partner is irresponsible, you are probably gnashing your teeth with efforts to change him or her to become more responsible.

Maybe he's irresponsible about money, or she is – getting hooked on impulse-buys or bingo or gambling (point 94) or a load of HP (point 77).

Or she seems to be rather casual about the children's welfare, leaving them free of supervision where you wouldn't.

We've seen in earlier points, however, that the desire to change the partner is basically the desire to make them more like you, to have your standards and way of looking at life and to worry about the same things you worry about.

If, for example, you are an insecure person, so that every financial risk or debt is a real threat to your peace of mind, you will desperately want your partner to have this particular fear too, for then he will be as cautious as you are and avoid all risk and debt.

And you will consider him 'irresponsible' – by your standards – if he is not like that. The slightest risk, even a small debt, means: 'He has no responsibility, he doesn't care'. And the truth is that he doesn't care in the same way as you do. He has none of your feelings on this matter. He has his own – perhaps more bold, less wise, but they are *there*.

Similarly, your feelings about letting the children have more independence may be quite different from his. He may think you 'irresponsible' to leave an 11-year-old in the house alone. He has his own unalterable feelings about the possible dangers – which you don't have. And he cannot share your unanxious, trusting feelings about this.

So, once more, you can only approach an answer or a compromise by getting these feelings and differences out in the open. It's no answer to take the irresponsibility as a cross you have to bear, or work away at the impossible task of making him or her change a whole outlook on life.

You can, instead, try to understand why he or she acts like this and accept the differences in your deepest feelings. You cannot alter the feelings but, once these have been understood, it's remarkable how willing most of us are to give up those ways of acting on our feelings which are disrupting our own lives or upsetting someone we value.

85 The leaning partner

The trouble is that most of us like both to lean and be leant on. Leaning on someone means you can hand over to them all the responsibilities for your happiness and look to them and them alone to satisfy all your needs.

Being leant on is also comfortable in some ways because it gives you power over the other person and allows you to direct his or her life according to your own wishes and not theirs. Which is very nice if you like controlling people.

Although we all have both these characteristics in us, some of us have an excessive amount of the wish to lean and others have an excessive amount of the wish to be leant on.

When it comes to choosing a marriage partner, these two different kinds of people are expert at unconsciously winkling each other out. And the partnership will remain stable, without serious conflicts, unless one of two things happens.

1 The leaning partner gains a degree of maturity and wants to be more independent and better at finding personal satisfactions.

A wife might, for example, stop feeling lonely when her husband is away on business by finding companionship among friends or becoming absorbed in an activity or hobby.

The only drawback here is that if her husband needs her to be dependent on him he might get a little shaken when she starts to have a mind of her own and becomes more equal. There is no answer here except for him to grow up too and enjoy an equal partnership instead of an unbalanced one.

Another difficulty here is that when a dependent person realizes that he or she is dependent, it creates resentment against the person leant on. There is hostility too when, as is inevitable, every need of the leaning partner is not met.

2 The alternative is when the partner who's leant on tires of the responsibility and demands and tries to shake the leaner off into an independent existence. This may be difficult. The leaner has had no practice.

But these are deep waters. They represent on both sides a childish way of loving, rooted in the 'unbalance' of power rather than in exchanges between equals. If your marriage looks like this, you need help.

But it's scarcely a problem to worry about if a partner is the leaner in some situations, the leaned-on in others. This is the way of most marriages, and expresses the presence in all of us of the wish to be dependent *and* independent.

part viii Crises in the Marriage

People often say that two adults ought to have the intelligence to sort out their own problems; and this view makes us feel rather ashamed to be in a crisis at all. It makes us doubly ashamed to be in need of help and to ask for it, or to read a book to get it.

But, of course, a crisis in a marriage has nothing to do with intelligence at all. It has all to do with feelings. And you can be very intelligent indeed, and so can your partner, but still be very lost in a welter of conflicting emotions that makes it quite impossible for you to sort out which road to take at a cross-roads.

Hurt, anger, sadness, feelings of being rejected or betrayed – all these blind you to seeing the reality of the situation and the way out. You can't see the wood for the trees, nor the love for all the hate. This is when help may be needed so that you can stand back, sort out your tangled emotions and see what really might be the best way out for you and your partner.

This part gives you some ideas about how to do that.

86 Cat and dog life

When a husband and wife are open enemies and engaged in a kind of mutual destruction, it has to be faced that it may not be possible to put things right.

For they may not want to. The ways in which they need to knock each other down – by needling or silences or witholding of every comfort and affection from each other – might have become so compulsive that they've lost all will to change things.

Anyone outside the marriage may, from sheer humanity, feel it is a great pity that two people should spend their lives like this instead of enjoying the warmth and affection they are both really needing. But it is their life. And unless they themselves can say: 'Look, we can't go on like this. Let's try and do something about it', no one can help.

So if you're either the cat or the dog and believe you're stuck with this rôle – well, you may not be. It's up to you. Even if you reckon it is 'not your fault' – and it certainly won't be wholly your fault –it can still be a step forward for you to get help towards seeing whether this mutual destruction can be halted or not.

A marriage guidance counsellor is the source of help for this. He or she also has legal and medical experts to help with the knottier problems in a marriage crisis.

87 'I want my freedom'

Sometimes I think the best move when a husband or wife is urgently waving a banner for freedom is to take them up on it.

'Right! When were you thinking of going – this evening or tomorrow? Shall I pack or will you? Now, let's make a list. Will you take your dog or shall we put him in kennels? Who does that clock belong to – I can't remember? Who paid for the typewriter? Is the record-player yours or mine?'

And so on. Beastly, I know, but it's one way of pointing up what an enormous number of small taken-for granted things make up the being-together of two people.

They are held together, it then seems, not so much by what they do and say but by this extra something they've made between them – a relationship and all its ancillaries, from children to family jokes, from sex to the same brand of toothpaste. The whole is greater than the sum of the parts. And it's a complex pattern, built up by us, which we cannot alter or tear apart without altering a great deal in ourselves.

So, whenever a partner contemplates 'being free' in one area – to sleep with whom he likes, for instance, – he's likely to find that this does not give him freedom from the whole pattern of his life.

So it's wise, when freedom is the cry, to isolate, if you can, what particular freedom is being called for. And tackle that. With help if necessary.

It may be that job or house is basically unsatisfactory and what's really wanted is a change, a break in monotony, a new challenge or a loosening of routine.

Shackles can be shed without breaking an entire marriage. And freedom can be found *in the marriage* if you take the trouble to examine together the factor that's making him or her feel restricted.

88 The partner who walks out

At the very least a sudden walk-out, without warning, is an untidy, selfish thing to do. At the worst it's an extremely cruel, punishing act towards someone who faces the same problem as you do – the breakdown of a marriage.

But what's the answer? It isn't much help, when things have reached this stage, to go straight round to where the partner's escaped to (if you know) and continue the battle on different ground.

It doesn't do much good either, except to relieve your anger, to 'tackle' the other man or woman to whom the partner may have escaped (although this always seems to be very tempting).

Better to accept, for the moment, that he or she has opted out of responsibilities and make sure that ordinary life can continue as well as possible without his or her presence.

For a deserted wife this means primarily money. Go to the Probation Officer about this and you'll be advised on how to attempt a reconciliation or obtain maintenance for you and the children.

If you're all right for money but are in an emotional turmoil about the walk-out, then you may still want to talk about it to a Probation Officer or marriage guidance counsellor and see how best to cope with the situation.

If it's the wife who's walked out, there may be no money problem but perhaps a worse one – the care of the home and children. Sometimes difficulties are overcome by the help of neighbours, having a relative to stay, or father and children moving in with another family or his parents.

The Welfare Department of the local authority or the Children's Officer can advise; but don't be frightened, as some deserted fathers are, that your children will automatically be taken into care. This will not be the case unless there is no *other way* for them to be looked after properly.

I'm not saying that if there's a walk-out you should just accept it as final. Obviously, if you want the marriage to survive, you'll do all you can to sort out the trouble with your partner. What I am saying is that, whether you're the husband or wife, you'll have more chance of getting over this and getting the family re-united if you keep calm, cope with the circumstances as they are and get the help you need.

If the partner has 'gone missing' completely and you want to trace him or her, see Appendix A for details under International Investigation.

89 'For the children's sake . . .'

A lot of marriages *do* weather bad patches and overcome

crises because there are children. And there's no doubt that one of the good reasons for keeping a marriage intact, in spite of difficulties, is the need of children for a united home with two parents in it.

But it's not a good reason for failing to tackle your difficulties. You may feel and have agreed that you are staying together 'for the children's sake' but, of course, this will not really benefit them or anybody else all that much if you don't also stay together in harmony.

If you're always at loggerheads about unresolved conflicts, this might harm the children more than living with one parent and visiting the other occasionally. But neither of these is the best that can be done for them – or for you.

So if you want to stay together in spite of very strong longings to part, then I do urge you to go a step further and decide to do something about the rifts between you.

In the rest of this book are ideas about the possible causes of the rift and how to tackle them.

90 When the children have gone

A warning's needed here. It's very easy to think that everything will fall into place when the children are 'off your hands'. You expect either that you will suddenly have enormous companionship – 'now we've really got time for each other' – or that your lives will be empty and flat.

One is an optimist's view, the other a pessimist's. The truth is neither. It will be as it has been before – only more so.

If you haven't had the habit of interest in each other's activities and feelings – I don't mean constant 'togetherness' – then it won't suddenly emerge because the children have left. What they leave behind, if you've no living relationship to speak of, is a vacuum.

But if you have had this real interest in the other as a person – the kind of interest which asks and listens and follows progress and sympathises with set-backs – it can be built-on when you're freer of the claims of the children.

This is merely another way of saying there'll be no crisis or loneliness if you love each other – but "love each other' precisely in this way of interest and understanding and concern.

This is over and above the sexual interest, the 'business partnership' in running the family, and the need, in some people, to be actually in each other's company to feel cherished.

If this kind of love hasn't been there before, then it's not too late to put it into your marriage now that you and your partner are alone. You need it more than ever before. You may, in fact, find that it has been there all the time and that now you have the opportunity to express it.

91 Separation

If you think legal separation is a good way out of your difficulties, you should approach the local Magistrates' Court. The grounds for separation are far more numerous than for divorce, so you may want to consult a solicitor about this, but a solicitor's help is not a necessity in getting a separation order.

Its advantages over divorce are the relative quickness of the proceedings, and the fact that maintenance orders resulting from it are more easily enforced. (A husband can be committed to prison for arrears of maintenance – which admittedly isn't much help to anyone – or his earnings can be attached, which means his employer is given the power to deduct part of his wages and send them to the court.)

But it does mean that many temporary upsets in a marriage get fought over in court and 'hardened' into bitter attitudes which might be better sorted out in privacy with the help of a social worker.

So it's worthwhile, if you're thinking of applying for a separation order, to have a word first with a probation officer, marriage guidance counsellor or anyone else you know who deals with marital problems.

An agreed informal separation, however, when wife and children go and stay with mother, or husband kips down somewhere else for a while, can be a help. When there have been heated emotions and quarrels, it can be a relief just to be free of the tensions between you.

It goes without saying that the separation needs to be welcome to both sides, and to be used to take a cool long-distance look at where you're heading and why, and not to gather up strength and ammunition for further battles.

The main point, when you're considering a holiday apart or a break from each other because of a crisis, is not to get panicky on the grounds that if he or she 'gets away' it will be for good.

If there is in truth so little left between you that once away from the married home, or in it alone, a partner wants to make this break permanent, then perhaps, in the long run, it is better to discover that this is the case.

But where there is a lot left which is, for the moment, completely clouded by the recriminations and hurt of the crisis, it can help to get out of the centre of the storm for a while and look at it from a distance. And if this doesn't help as much as you thought, it would be wise to follow it up with some detached guidance.

92 Divorce

If you want a divorce, the first thing to do is to go to a solicitor. If you don't know of one, ask the Citizens' Advice Bureau. They will also tell you there about Legal Aid, whether you qualify for this or not, and which solicitors operate the scheme.

If you're thinking about divorce and want to get the grounds straight in your mind, you could consult a solicitor about this too, for a small fee and without any obligation to carry on with the suit. You could refer to any up-to-date book on family law in your local library. There are also one or two current paper-backs on the subject always on the market.

As divorce laws in England are in the process of being changed, it's not possible to give you the latest information here.

But you may be thinking about divorce and aren't sure whether you want one or not. In this case, a Probation Officer or marriage guidance counsellor will help.

Don't get the feeling that their job is to 'talk you out of wanting a divorce'. They're not in the least concerned to persuade you to stay married if it's not what you want. All they do is help you to find out what you and your partner really *do* want, and make your own decisions on that basis.

part ix Help Wanted

This part is about marriage problems which are so grave and worrying that one partner has to send out an SOS to the outside world. Fortunately there is now some source of help for all these problems, either 'official' or voluntary. I do urge you to use them.

93 The alcoholic

Anyone who drinks to such excess that his health is affected, and his relationships and family life are disturbed, is nowadays recognised as being 'sick' and in need of help.

Sometimes an alcoholic wants to beat the habit and is willing to get help for himself. He can get National Health treatment through his own doctor. Or he can contact the Alcoholism Information Centre, 25 Wincott Street, London, SE11 for information on what treatment and help is available.

Or he can apply to Alcoholics Anonymous, 11 Redcliffe, Gardens, London, SW10 which runs self-help groups throughout the country in which members support each other in their efforts to achieve freedom from the drinking habit.

Where the alcoholic is not himself willing to get help, both these organisations will advise or help his wife, other relatives or friends. There are women alcoholics too, of course; where I have said 'he' you can substitute 'she'. The same help is available.

94 The gambler

If you're worried by a gambling partner, whether your wife's always at the Bingo hall or your husband's got a second home at the betting shop, it might help first to untangle your feelings about this.

Gambling has always been looked on as a 'sin' in our culture, and although it's now socially acceptable (but not to everybody) and brings in a lot of government revenue, we do still retain a bit of this feeling that it's wicked and irresponsible to chance your arm and take risks with your money (even if we do it ourselves).

You could allow for this feeling and then calmly consider whether your partner's 'little flutters' are actually disrupting the budget or doing any harm. Be honest about this and don't let your dislike of the whole thing colour the *facts*.

If it isn't, and it's part of your partner's life that evidently gives him or her pleasure – and is not his or her whole life – then perhaps there's an answer in accepting that you have a different attitude to it. Neither of you *can* change the other, so you might as well realize the difference is *there* and live with it. It's not a case of enduring what can't be cured, but of understanding it and seeing that cure docsn't come into it, anymore than it would if you had blue eyes and he had brown.

But where gambling is taking a hold of someone's entire life and is in danger of beggaring him and his family, then help is needed. The organisation to get in touch with, for either the gambler or his relatives, is: Gamblers Anonymous, 19 Abbey House, Victoria Street, London, SW1.

95 Physical illness

When a husband or wife is chronically ill and needs care and some nursing attention at home, it can lead to a certain amount of emotional strain as well as practical difficulties.

But there are any number of organisations, specialising in different forms of chronic illness, which exist to relieve this strain a little. They have rounded up all the information about facilities and social provisions available – such as extra bedding or nourishment and, in some cases, they help with cash grants for nursing, convalescence and home comforts.

Some organisations also help by putting the relatives of sick or handicapped adults and children in touch with each other. This is often just what's needed by husbands or wives who have become rather 'isolated' by their apparently unique worries.

The list of these organisations is too long to print here. But the main ones – covering such illnesses as cancer, chest and heart diseases, epilepsy and muscular dystrophy – can be found in the Consumer's Guide to the Social Services by Phyllis Willmott (Pelican) 6s.

There is also a comprehensive list in a booklet published by The Patients Association. It costs 2s 6d (including postage) from the Associations' officers at 335 Grey's Inn Road, London WC1 and is called 'Organisations Concerned with Particular Diseases or Handicaps'.

96 Mental illness

Where mental illness is suspected, the first person for either partner to see, whether it's the sufferer or the other partner, is the family doctor. Only he can say if psychiatric help is needed and refer the patient, if necessary, to a clinic, hospital or psychiatrist.

Here's an important point: the fear of mental illness is often greater than the illness itself. This sometimes makes people feel much worse and actually prevents them getting help when it's needed.

Many forms of depression and anxiety states can be treated by the family doctor himself and, of course, the prospects of complete cure are much brighter if you don't delay in getting help.

For any family with a mentally ill member there's help available from the psychiatric social worker attached to the clinic or hospital or practice where the 'patient' is under treatment or has been having treatment.

If there is no social worker of this kind in your area – and they are rather thin on the ground – and you need help and guidance, you can ask the Mental Welfare Office of your local authority, or you could write for information to the National Association for Mental Health, 39 Queen Anne Street, London, W1.

The booklet I mentioned in the last point, 'Organisations Concerned with Particular Diseases or Handicaps', also includes a list of organisations which help the mentally disturbed and their relatives.

People in despair or with thoughts of suicide can receive support and help from the well-known Samaritans. You will find your local branch, if there is one, advertised in your local paper or in the telephone directory.

In other emergencies, such as when a mentally disturbed partner has a relapse and needs expert assistance, the person to ring up is the Mental Welfare Officer, or the police (who will know where to contact him).

Former psychiatric patients can get support and social contact during their adjustment to ordinary life in Neurotics Nomine, which has some local branches. Details from Neurotics Nomine, 38 Marlborough Place, London NW8.

97 Up against the law

When a married man or woman tangles with the law and lands

up under supervision or in prison, it's now well-recognised that this may punish his or her partner and family almost as much, if not more, than it punishes the offender.

For this reason, various forms of help are available for the parents of delinquent children or the wives of prisoners. Your local Probation Officer is the person to ask about what help is available.

There are also several groups in existence for giving assistance to the wives of prisoners to cope with their difficulties, both practical and emotional. One, in London, is the Prisoners Wives Service, 378 Lillie Road, SW6.

If you want to find out if there is such a group in your area, or if there's a possibility of forming one, ask the Probation Officer. This Officer is also the person to ask for help in any marriage problem connected with the courts, the police or law-breaking.

98 Drugs

Drug addiction is not widespread as a *marriage* problem, mainly because dependence on drugs largely arises in emotionally-isolated people who have not been able to make any satisfying relationships.

But it can and has emerged as a problem *for* many marriages when a teenage son or daughter begins to experiment with drugs or is found to be addicted.

If you are wondering how to cope and need help and information you'd do well to get in touch with the Association for the Prevention of Addiction which has local branches and is hoping to start many more. It also has a referral centre manned by a psychologist. The address is in Appendix A.

99 Compulsive affairs

If your partner is constantly falling in love or having affairs there is only one way of looking at it which is capable of solving it in the end; that is, that this is not your problem alone (nor his alone, but a problem for *both* of you).

Now either one can get help. The promiscuous partner is probably less aware of the need for help for he or she is temporarily getting his or her needs from life in extra-marital entanglements. So it is usually the 'wronged' partner who will more willingly go to a doctor, marriage guidance counsellor or social worker.

Sometimes there's an additional problem in that a child is

conceived outside the marriage. In the case of an illegitimate child of the husband's, he will, of course, be liable to maintain the child.

When the wife conceives by a man other than her husband, she may not truly know if it is her husband's or the other man's until the child is born and perhaps not even then.

This is an appalling dilemma to be worrying over during pregnancy and the way out which seems least hurtful to anyone is for the wife to share the worry first, not with her husband, but with some detached expert who can help her to make up her own mind about telling her husband.

If the child is definitely illegitimate but help is needed with adoption, or with any other problem arising from the situation, the organisation to contact is The National Council for the Unmarried Mother and Her Child, 255 Kentish Town Road, London, NW5. They offer help to married mothers of illegitimate children as well as the unmarried.

100 Sexual deviation

It's as well to realise that a great deal of what one partner may consider deviant behaviour in the other partner can be well inside the norm.

Nevertheless, there is still a problem in that this behaviour, although not abnormal, is distressing. Some wives, for example, get extremely upset by their husbands' interest in strip-tease shows, pornographic pictures or erotic literature and consider this interest abnormal and therefore somewhat degrading for both partners.

These feelings are tied-up with much deeper feelings about sex and love. They very often include the inability to realise that these two things, love and sex, can be sharply separated in a man's mind. So there is seldom an answer in rational explanations by the husband or anyone else.

Sometimes a little more education about human nature can help (see the reading-list in Appendix B). But mostly the answer is the opportunity to recognise the feelings behind these worries in the presence of an understanding and trained listener – which means your doctor (if he has the time) or a marriage guidance counsellor.

But sometimes the deviation is unmistakable. There is, for example, the woman who has married a man who admits to homosexual tendencies and both have hoped that marriage will 'cure' him. They may have then found that it has not.

Or either partner will discover in the other, or in themselves, homosexual leanings which they can neither suppress nor come to terms with. There are also problems about transvestism (when either has a compulsion to wear the clothes of the opposite sex) or doubts in either the wife or husband about his or her true sex.

All these problems are what are known as psychosexual problems and need help. This is available from an organisation which deals primarily with homosexual problems (for both sexes) but also offers counselling, guidance or referral for any psychosexual problem in all age-groups. This is the Albany Trust, 32 Shaftesbury Avenue, London, W1. The help is confidential, of course, and to this end visits are by appointment only.

101 Loneliness

Although a husband or wife can be very lonely indeed, even in the presence of the partner, it's fortunately in their power to do something about this by improving their lines of communication or by finding other means within themselves to alleviate the sense of loneliness. (See points 4, 7, 10, 22, 80, and 82).

However, we should perhaps accept that a now-and-again sense of loneliness is an integral part of being a human being.

But when a partner dies, there can be acute loneliness and with it a very real fear that the sense of loss is going to last for ever. This makes some widows and widowers, especially if they are comparatively young, fling themselves into new friendships and other activities to fill the gap which they fear is permanent.

Then they often suffer feelings of guilt because their ability to find some pleasure in life seems to indicate that their sorrow was not real. And so they swing from one emotion to the other, first needing interests and companions, then feeling treacherous when they enjoy them.

Well, one can best help people in this situation by saying simply that grief takes time. We do need to mourn people we lose and follow our own pace for recovery. A natural part of this mourning is to feel remorse ('I could have done more for him/her') and to resist the idea of being happy again, as if it were a form of betrayal. All these feelings pass and you have no need to deny them or hide them.

So your loneliness will be less acute, perhaps, if you take your cue from your own feelings and not from any idea about how you ought to be feeling or behaving.

For help with any practical problems of widowhood, there is a pamphlet obtainable from Citizens Advice Bureaux for 3d. And to alleviate the feeling of loneliness, there are a number of Cruse Clubs for widows in various localities. For details write to Cruse Clubs, 6 Lion Gate Gardens, Richmond, Surrey.

Appendices

Appendix A Helping Agencies

PROBATION OFFICER

He (or she) helps with marital problems of all kinds but is, generally speaking, more concerned with problems arising out of court procedures, or the possibility of them, e.g. separation orders, maintenance, probationary supervision and delinquent minors.

To be found by enquiring at the Magistrates' Court or Town Hall – or ask a policeman.

MARRIAGE GUIDANCE COUNSELLOR

Counsellors are not paid but are carefully selected and trained for their work in helping with any problem in marriage or in relationships generally. They also have professional experts to consult when necessary.

Look under Marriage Guidance Council in the telephone book. Or write for the whereabouts of your nearest counsellor to the National Marriage Guidance Council, 58 Queen Anne St., London W1.

FAMILY PLANNING CLINICS

Contraceptive advice given and appliances supplied. A small fee is charged and you pay for the goods. Also help with subfertility in some Clinics and, in a few, help with sexual problems other than family planning. Any clinic will tell you which clinics give these forms of help. Or write for information to the Family Planning Association, 231 Tottenham Court Road, London W1.

THE ALBANY TRUST

(For help with psychosexual problems see point 100) 32 Shaftesbury Avenue, London W1. Visits by appointment only, so write or ring first.

FAMILY DISCUSSION BUREAU

Counselling/psychotherapy given to marriages in difficulties – mostly by referral from other helping agencies but also for a limited number of people who come to them of their own accord. The address is 2 Beaumont St, London W1.

CHILDREN'S OFFICER
Helps with any difficulty involving the welfare of children. And with fostering and adoption. Can be located at the offices of your County Council.

STANDING CONFERENCE OF SOCIETIES REGISTERED FOR ADOPTION
Gort Lodge, Petersham, Hants (see point 60). Supplies information about adoption and a list of adoption societies in a leaflet obtainable from this address. Price 1s plus 4d for postage.

AGNOSTICS ADOPTION SOCIETY (see point 60),
69 Chaucer Road, London, SE24.

HOUSEWIVES REGISTER
(see point 80). A way for house-bound wives 'with liberal interests' to keep in touch with each other through visits, newsletters and occasional conferences. 400 groups comprising about 7,000 youngish wives. National Organiser: Mrs. Jane Watt, Rowanbank, Gratham Road, Bottesford, Notts.

PRE-SCHOOL PLAYGROUPS ASSOCIATION
87A Borough High Street, London SE1 (see point 80). For information and practical guidance in forming a young children's play-group in your area.

INTERNATIONAL INVESTIGATION
(see point 88). 110 Middlesex St., London E1. This branch of the Salvation Army will try to trace any missing relative *except* missing husbands and putative fathers.

FAMILY SERVICES DEPARTMENT
280 Mare St., London E8. This Salvation Army department helps with tracing missing husbands and putative fathers.

CITIZENS' ADVICE BUREAU
For any problem under the sun. If they cannot give you the answers, they will tell you who can. Your local bureau's address will be in the telephone book and displayed on the noticeboard in your main Post Office.

THE SAMARITANS (see point 96).
Counselling and befriending for anyone lonely, in despair or

contemplating suicide. Contact is made by telephone which is manned round the clock. Your local service, if any, will be in the 'phone book and advertised in the local paper. If there isn't one, ring Mansion 9000 if it's urgent. For information on your nearest branch, write to The Secretary, 11F Western Road, Beckenham, Kent.

ALCOHOLICS ANONYMOUS (see point 93)
11 Redcliffe Gardens, London SW10.

ALCOHOLISM INFORMATION CENTRE (see point 93)
25 Wincott St., London SE11.

GAMBLERS ANONYMOUS (see point 94)
19 Abbey House, Victoria St., SW1.

NATIONAL ASSOCIATION FOR MENTAL HEALTH (see point 96)
39 Queen Anne St., London W1.

NEUROTICS NOMINE (see point 96)
38 Marlborough Place, London NW8.

ASSOCIATION FOR THE PREVENTION OF ADDICTION (see point 98).
24 Cranbourn St., London WC2.

NATIONAL COUNCIL FOR THE UNMARRIED MOTHER AND HER CHILD (see point 99).
255 Kentish Town Road, London NW5.

CRUSE CLUBS (see point 101)
6 Lion Gate Gardens, Richmond, Surrey.

Appendix B Further Reading

Most of these books are available both at bookshops and by post. Books available by post have the postal charge as well as the price given with the title.

Except where another address is given, all the books available by post can be bought from The Book Shop, National Marriage Guidance Council, 58 Queen Anne Street, London W1.

GENERAL

Thinking About Marriage J. H. Wallis Penguin 3s 6d (8d). An experienced counsellor talks about marriage as a personal relationship.

The Art of Marriage Dr Mary Macaulay Delisle 3s 6d (8d) Covers all aspects, particularly the physical.

Middle-Aged Marriage NMGC 2s 6d (6d)

THE OUTSIDE WORLD

101 Points on buying a House Dickens Press 3s 6d (4d)

101 Ways to Manage Your Money Edward Leader Dickens Press 3s 6d (4d)

The £ s d of Marriage NMGC 3s 6d (6d)

Consumer's Guide to the British Social Services Pyllis Willmott Penguin 6s (8)

SEX

Help with Sex Problems in Marriage NMGC 3s 6d (6d)

Sex the Plain Facts Dr James Bevan Faber 10s 6d (8d)

Modern Contraception Dr. Philip M. Bloom Delisle 2s 6d

THE FAMILY

Baby and Child Care Dr Benjamin Spock New English Library 7s 6d (9d)

The Child, the Family and the Outside World Dr D. Winnicott Penguin 4s 6d (8d)

What Shall I Tell My Child? Central Council for Mental Health 1s 3d (6d)

15 Plus Facts of Life Kenneth Barnes BMA 1s 6d (6d)

Parents Under Stress NMGC 3s 6d (6d) (see point 73)

Organisations concerned with Particular Diseases and Handicaps. From: The Patients Association, 335 Greys Inn Road, London WC1 2s 6d (inc. post) (see points 95 and 96).

Index

Numbers refer to Points, not pages. Letters refer to Appendices.

inside information books

These books have been specially planned to provide the latest information and up-to-date advice on the most important problems affecting the family in contemporary society

Each book has been written by a specialist or consultant, familiar with the problems the reader would put to him

Marriage

conflict in marriage. Angela Willans BA, a leading writer on personal relationships, in close touch with the Marriage Guidance Council, offers help with the more serious problems between marriage partners

sex and birth control. Dr Rosalie Taylor, family planning specialist, medical officer to the Marie Stopes Memorial Centre and the Family Planning Association, makes a comprehensive survey of the sexual relationship and explains choice, suitability and use of the present day methods of contraception

Parenthood

understanding infants (birth to pre-school). Martha Harris B.A., child psycho-therapist at the Tavistock Clinic, discusses the growth of relationships between parents and infants and advises on the main problems they may encounter with each other

parents' problems with children (6 to 13). A. D. Wooster BA, child psychologist at Nottingham University, gives practical advice on the relationship between parents and schoolchildren and the main problems of upbringing

Education

educational choice. Edwin Packer, former problems expert at the Advisory Centre for Education, explains comprehensively the many options available to parents and their children and the consequences of their decisions *career opportunities*. J. C. Tomlinson and Janet Moggridge of the Careers Research and Advisory Centre, Cambridge, assist parents of school leavers and advanced students in making educational and career decisions

solving career problems. J. J. Q. Fox MA MSc, an occupational psychology consultant, provides parents, school leavers and graduates with systematic methods of analysing abilities and interests to reach sound decisions about career development

careers in management. H. Johannsen, of the British Institute of Management, explains to those who aim at an executive career the nature of modern business management and how to attain the opportunities offered

Family affairs

the family and the law. Stephen Bristow LLB explains the laws affecting marriage, parenthood, the home, finance, liability, employment, wills etc. a knowledge of which is essential under modern social conditions

tax and insurance. Oliver Stanley MA (Oxon) and David Ross MA LLB, former Tax Inspectors, give practical advice on how to obtain the maximum reliefs from tax on personal and business incomes

W. A. Dinsdale PhD, the insurance expert and writer, explains an insurance plan for all basic personal and family responsibilities

pre-retirement and retirement. J. P. McErlean L ès L, who has lectured for the Pre-retirement Association, City Literary Institute, Morley College and numerous industrial firms, explains the personal and financial implications of retirement and provides advice on practical planning

5s each